7th Workshop on Cognitive Aspects of Computational Language Learning (CogACLL 2016)

Held at ACL 2016

Berlin, Germany
11 August 2016

ISBN: 978-1-5108-2775-2

ACL 2016

The 54th Annual Meeting of the Association for Computational Linguistics

Proceedings of the 7th Workshop on Cognitive Aspects of Computational Language Learning

August 11, 2016
Berlin, Germany

Introduction

The 7th Workshop on Cognitive Aspects of Computational Language Learning (CogACLL) took place on August 11, 2016 in Berlin, Germany, in conjunction with the ACL 2016. The workshop was endorsed by ACL Special Interest Group on Natural Language Learning (SIGNLL). This is the seventh edition of related workshops first held with ACL 2007, EACL 2009, 2012 and 2014, EMNLP 2015, and as a standalone event in 2013.

The workshop is targeted at anyone interested in the relevance of computational techniques for understanding first, second and bilingual language acquisition and change or loss in normal and pathological conditions.

The human ability to acquire and process language has long attracted interest and generated much debate due to the apparent ease with which such a complex and dynamic system is learnt and used on the face of ambiguity, noise and uncertainty. This subject raises many questions ranging from the nature vs. nurture debate of how much needs to be innate and how much needs to be learned for acquisition to be successful, to the mechanisms involved in this process (general vs specific) and their representations in the human brain. There are also developmental issues related to the different stages consistently found during acquisition (e.g. one word vs. two words) and possible organizations of this knowledge. These have been discussed in the context of first and second language acquisition and bilingualism, with cross linguistic studies shedding light on the influence of the language and the environment.

The past decades have seen a massive expansion in the application of statistical and machine learning methods to natural language processing (NLP). This work has yielded impressive results in numerous speech and language processing tasks, including e.g. speech recognition, morphological analysis, parsing, lexical acquisition, semantic interpretation, and dialogue management. The good results have generally been viewed as engineering achievements. However, researchers have also investigated the relevance of computational learning methods for research on human language acquisition and change. The use of computational modeling has been boosted by advances in machine learning techniques, and the availability of resources like corpora of child and child-directed sentences, and data from psycholinguistic tasks by normal and pathological groups. Many of the existing computational models attempt to study language tasks under cognitively plausible criteria (such as memory and processing limitations that humans face), and to explain the developmental stages observed in the acquisition and evolution of the language abilities. In doing so, computational modeling provides insight into the plausible mechanisms involved in human language processes, and inspires the development of better language models and techniques. These investigations are very important since if computational techniques can be used to improve our understanding of human language acquisition and change, these will not only benefit cognitive sciences in general but will reflect back to NLP and place us in a better position to develop useful language models.

We invited submissions on relevant topics, including:

- Computational learning theory and analysis of language learning and organization

- Computational models of first, second and bilingual language acquisition

- Computational models of language changes in clinical conditions

- Computational models and analysis of factors that influence language acquisition and use in different age groups and cultures

- Computational models of various aspects of language and their interaction effect in acquisition, processing and change

- Computational models of the evolution of language

- Data resources and tools for investigating computational models of human language processes

- Empirical and theoretical comparisons of the learning environment and its impact on language processes

- Cognitively oriented Bayesian models of language processes

- Computational methods for acquiring various linguistic information (related to e.g. speech, morphology, lexicon, syntax, semantics, and discourse) and their relevance to research on human language acquisition

- Investigations and comparisons of supervised, unsupervised and weakly-supervised methods for learning (e.g. machine learning, statistical, symbolic, biologically-inspired, active learning, various hybrid models) from a cognitive perspective.

Acknowledgements

We would like to thank the members of the Program Committee for the timely reviews and the authors for their valuable contributions. Aline Villavicencio is partly funded by projects from Samsung Eletrônica da Amazônia Ltda, and from CNPq (482520/2012-4, 312114/2015-0). Alessandro Lenci by project CombiNet (PRIN 2010-11 20105B3HE8) funded by the Italian Ministry of Education, University and Research (MIUR).

Anna Korhonen
Alessandro Lenci
Brian Murphy
Thierry Poibeau
Aline Villavicencio

Organizers:

Anna Korhonen, University of Cambridge (UK)
Alessandro Lenci, University of Pisa (Italy)
Brian Murphy, Queen's University Belfast (UK)
Thierry Poibeau, LATTICE-CNRS (France)
Aline Villavicencio, Federal University of Rio Grande do Sul (Brazil)

Program Committee:

Dora Alexopoulou, University of Cambridge (UK)
Afra Alishahi, Tilburg University (Netherlands)
Colin Bannard, University of Liverpool (UK)
Robert Berwick, Massachusetts Institute of Technology (USA)
Philippe Blache, LPL-CNRS (France)
Antal van den Bosch, Radboud University Nijmegen (Netherlands)
Chris Brew, Thomson Reuters (UK)
Grzegorz Chrupala, Saarland University (Germany)
Alexander Clark, Royal Holloway, University of London (UK)
Robin Clark, University of Pennsylvania (USA)
Walter Daelemans, University of Antwerp (Belgium)
Dan Dediu, Max Planck Institute for Psycholinguistics (The Netherlands)
Barry Devereux, University of Cambridge (UK)
Emmanuel Dupoux, ENS - CNRS (France)
Afsaneh Fazly, University of Toronto (Canada)
Marco Idiart, Federal University of Rio Grande do Sul (Brazil)
Gianluca Lebani, University of Pisa (Italy)
Igor Malioutov, Massachusetts Institute of Technology (USA)
Tim O'Donnel, Massachusetts Institute of Technology (USA)
Muntsa Padró, Holmes Semantic Solutions (France)
Lisa Pearl, University of California - Irvine (USA)
Ari Rappoport, The Hebrew University of Jerusalem (Israel)
Sabine Schulte im Walde, University of Stuttgart (Germany)
Ekaterina Shutova, University of Cambridge (UK)
Maity Siqueira, Federal University of Rio Grande do Sul (Brazil)
Mark Steedman, University of Edinburgh (UK)
Suzanne Stevenson, University of Toronto (Canada)
Remi van Trijp, Sony Computer Science Laboratory Paris (France)
Shuly Wintner, University of Haifa (Israel)
Charles Yang, University of Pennsylvania (USA)
Menno van Zaanen, Tilburg University (Netherlands)
Alessandra Zarcone, University of Stuttgart (Germany)

Table of Contents

Conference Program

Thursday, August 11, 2016

9:00–9:05   *Welcome and Opening Session*

9:05–9:35   **Session 1 - Language in Clinical Conditions**

9:05–9:35   *Automated Discourse Analysis of Narrations by Adolescents with Autistic Spectrum Disorder*
Michaela Regneri and Diane King

9:35–10:30   *Invited Speaker I*

10:30–11:00   *Coffee Break*

11:00–11:30   **Poster Session**

11:00–11:30   *Detection of Alzheimer's disease based on automatic analysis of common objects descriptions*
Laura Hernandez-Dominguez, Edgar Garcia-Cano, Sylvie Ratté and Gerardo Sierra Martínez

11:00–11:30   *Conversing with the elderly in Latin America: a new cohort for multimodal, multilingual longitudinal studies on aging*
Laura Hernandez-Dominguez, Sylvie Ratté, Boyd Davis and Charlene Pope

11:00–11:30   *Leveraging Annotators' Gaze Behaviour for Coreference Resolution*
Joe Cheri, Abhijit Mishra and Pushpak Bhattacharyya

11:00–11:30   *From alignment of etymological data to phylogenetic inference via population genetics*
Javad Nouri and Roman Yangarber

11:00–11:30   *An incremental model of syntactic bootstrapping*
Christos Christodoulopoulos, Dan Roth and Cynthia Fisher

Thursday, August 11, 2016 (continued)

11:30–12:30   Session 2: Child Directed Language

11:30–12:00   *Longitudinal Studies of Variation Sets in Child-directed Speech*
Mats Wirén, Kristina Nilsson Björkenstam, Gintaré Grigonyté and Elisabet Eir Cortes

12:00–12:30   *Learning Phone Embeddings for Word Segmentation of Child-Directed Speech*
Jianqiang Ma, Çağrı Çöltekin and Erhard Hinrichs

12:30–14:00   *Lunch Break*

14:00–15:00   *Invited Talk II*

15:00–15:30   Session 3: Learning Artificial Languages

15:00–15:30   *Generalization in Artificial Language Learning: Modelling the Propensity to Generalize*
Raquel Garrido Alhama and Willem Zuidema

15:30–16:00   *Coffee Break*

16:00–17:00   Session 4: Language Acquisition

16:00–16:30   *Explicit Causal Connections between the Acquisition of Linguistic Tiers: Evidence from Dynamical Systems Modeling*
Daniel Spokoyny, Jeremy Irvin and Fermin Moscoso del Prado Martin

16:30–17:00   *Modelling the informativeness and timing of non-verbal cues in parent-child interaction*
Kristina Nilsson Björkenstam, Mats Wirén and Robert Östling

Automated Discourse Analysis of Narrations by Adolescents with Autistic Spectrum Disorder

Michaela Regneri
IT Department
SPIEGEL-Verlag
Hamburg, Germany
michaela.regneri@spiegel.de

Diane King
National Foundation for
Educational Research (NFER)
London, United Kingdom
d.king@nfer.ac.uk

Abstract

We present a study about automated discourse analysis of oral narrative language in adolescents with autistic spectrum disorder (ASD). The basis of this evaluation is an existing dataset of fictional narrations of individuals with ASD and two matched comparison groups. We use three robust measures for quantifying different aspects of text cohesion on this corpus. These measures and several combinations of them correlate strongly with human cohesion annotations. Our evaluation will show which of these also distinguish the ASD group from the two comparison groups, which do not, and which differences are related to language competence rather than to factors specific to ASD.

1 Introduction

Language is, in many ways, a window to the mind. Written or spoken utterances convey much more than their content – they also provide information about the person who is writing or speaking the respective words. The research field of computational stylometry is concerned with the analysis of (written or transcribed) text and how it reveals information about the person who has produced this (see Daelemans (2013) for an overview). Typical applications, often with a focus on frequently updated websites and social media, are automated authorship attribution, gender distinction or forensic purposes.

A growing and very interesting subfield of computational stylometry is the detection of idiosyncratic language which may be found in individuals who have cognitive, affective or developmental disorders: while standard stylometry uses mostly focus on the pure identification of certain users or user groups, often with hardly interpretable features (like function word use), diagnostic analysis has the additional goal of making sense out of the actual features. The hope here is to gain more insight into the underlying disorder by analysing how it affects language. Additionally, there are also systems that automatically can identify or predict the onset of the condition in question.

Our focus is on the diagnostic analysis of oral narratives produced by adolescents with autistic spectrum disorder (ASD). ASD is a neurodevelopmental disorder characterised by impairment in social communication and restricted, repetitive and stereotyped patterns of behaviour (American Psychiatric Association, 2013). Although the social and communication difficulties of individuals with ASD have been well documented, little is known about narrative language in this population: whilst there has been a great deal of research on ASD by psychologists and neurologists, there are not many corpus analyses to support assumptions on language development and ASD. We are particularly interested in discourse cohesion, with cohesion being defined as the way in which devices are used to link together sentences, clauses and propositions. This includes the sequencing of and transitions between each event in a narrative. Although the production of a cohesive narrative is reported to be challenging for individuals with ASD, there is only limited work on systematic corpus analyses, mainly due to the lack suitable datasets.

Our work is based on a recently published dataset of fictional narratives told by young people with ASD (King et al., 2014). We expressly do not aim to just automatically identify stories from an ASD group, because that would be easily accomplished using crude features like story length. Our goal is instead to find meaningful cohesion-related features that distinguish the language of individuals wth ASD.

1

Proceedings of the 7th Workshop on Cognitive Aspects of Computational Language Learning, pages 1–9,
Berlin, Germany, August 11, 2016. ©2016 Association for Computational Linguistics

Our contribution is threefold: First, we present robust measures that allow the automated assessment of cohesion in short texts, and introduce skewness as a new measure for coreference chains. Second, we show which features of the text cohesion we measure are ASD-specific according to our data, and which are related to language competence. Lastly, we also show the correlation of our measures with human judgments of story cohesion.

2   Related Work

Many automated approaches to diagnostic analysis detect Alzheimer's and related forms of dementia: there are extensive studies on the specific language changes in people that develop dementia (Hirst and Wei Feng, 2012; Le et al., 2011), showing how the syntactic complexity of sentences declines with the disease's progress. Some classifiers are capable of automated diagnosis from continuous speech (Baldas et al., 2011), and, additionally, the "Nun study" resulted in a system that can predict whether or not an individual will develop Alzheimer's decades before the actual onset of cognitive decline (Riley et al., 2005).

Other systems recognize spontaneous speech by individuals with more general mild cognitive impairments, for adults (Roark et al., 2011) and also for children (Gabani et al., 2009). Hong et al. (2012) present an unusual study on the language of adult patients with schizophrenia.

Previous research on narratives of children with ASD has reported difficulties with both structural and evaluative language. Individuals with ASD struggle with expressing sentiment and make fewer references to mental states than their typically developing peers (Capps et al., 2000; Tager-Flusberg, 1996). However, other experiments show that, when carefully matched with comparison groups on cognitive and language ability, many of these differences are not evident.

More basic problems emanate from a general lower syntactic complexity (Tager-Flusberg and Sullivan, 1995) and difficulties in producing a coherent narrative. Karmiloff-Smith (1985) argues that the production of a coherent narrative is dependent on the integration of knowledge of both coherence and cohesion; coherence being defined as the structure of a story and cohesion as the devices used to link together sentences, clauses and propositions, thereby maintaining a common

theme. Loveland and Tunali (1993) found that individuals with autism were less likely to tell a story as a coherent sequence and more likely to produce narratives that included bizarre, unrelated or inappropriate material. Diehl et al. (2006) also report that narratives produced by individuals with ASD were significantly less coherent than those of a comparison group. However, Tager-Flusberg and Sullivan (1995) found no significant differences in the use of lexical cohesion devices between three groups of children with autism, learning disabilities and typically developing, matched on verbal mental age.

Some of these language difficulties have been subject to automated analysis: Prud'hommeaux et al. (2011) analyzed data of very young children (6-7 years old). They built an automated classifier that distinguished sentences uttered by children with ASD from sentences of two control groups (one with children with a language-impairment, one with typically developing children). The authors themselves note some drawbacks of their underlying dataset, in particular that some children in the ASD group were also classified as language-impaired. In consequence, a clear distinction between these groups was impossible.

In two follow-up studies (Rouhizadeh et al., 2013; Rouhizadeh et al., 2015), the authors analysed whole narratives (retellings) told by children (mean age 6.4) with ASD compared to a typically developing control group (with the same average age and IQ). As discourse-related measures, they use the tf-idf measure (Luhn, 1957) and several measures of text similarity to identify idiosyncratic words and topics. The texts from the control group and some crowdsourced retellings from typically developing adults served as a basis for determining unusualness.

Regneri and King (2015) present a study on a much larger dataset with non-fictional stories about everyday scenarios (like *having a birthday* or *being angry*). Next to several shallow language features, they also evaluate tf-idf and show that this is actually more closely related to language competence than to ASD. However, they do not evaluate any other discourse-related features.

For our study, we use a dataset with fictional stories, and take the discourse-level investigation a step further: we present different measures of text cohesion, which quantify some actually ASD-specific difficulties with narrative.

| | Forest | | | |
Group	ASD	Lang.	Age	All
Cohesion	1.79	2.93	2.76	2.00
Sent. / Story	7.64	9.07	10.10	8.86
Words / Sent.	10.46	12.19	11.37	11.40

| | Mountain | | | |
Group	ASD	Lang.	Age	All
Cohesion	2.21	2.96	3.04	2.49
Sent. / Story	10.00	9.90	12.39	10.62
Words / Sent.	10.59	10.57	10.98	10.71

| | All Stories | | | |
Group	ASD	Lang.	Age	All
Cohesion	2.00	2.95	2.90	2.24
Sent. / Story	8.88	9.49	11.24	9.76
Words / Sent.	10.54	11.33	11.15	11.01

Table 1: Manually assigned cohesion scores, average story and sentence lengths for the corpus.

3 Data

We base our analysis on a dataset collected by King et al. (2014), which we describe in more detail in the following. The corpus contains transcripts of fictional stories constructed by the children after one of two different prompts. Appendix A shows some examples from the story collection. King et al. also report extensive manual annotation of the narratives, parts of which we will use as a gold standard for our automated experiments.

3.1 Data collection

The participants were divided in three groups: 27 high functioning adolescents with ASD aged 11 to 14 years, one comparison group of 27 adolescents matched with the ASD group on chronological age and nonverbal ability, and a second comparison group of 27 children and adolescents aged between 7 and 14 years, who were individually matched with the ASD group on a measure of expressive language (Recalling Sentences subtest of the CELF IV (Semel et al., 2006)) and on non-verbal ability. All groups had average scores on non-verbal and verbal measures, as measured by the Matrices test of the BAS II (Elliot et al., 1996) and the BPVS II (Dunn and Dunn, 1997). There were no significant differences between the groups

in measures of non-verbal ability, verbal ability or expressive language. The average age difference between the language-matched control group and the two other groups is 17 months.

Participants in all three groups were presented with two story stems and asked to continue the narrative. Each story stem was accompanied with a picture illustrating each prompt. The development of these materials was based on the work of Stein and Albro (1997), but adapted to be more suitable for the age group of this study. To prevent order effects, the presentation of the story stems was counterbalanced. After one practice story, each participant completed the following two story stems:

1. The "forest" story:

   The boy ran into the forest. He looked ahead of him and saw a little green man in a spaceship.

2. The "mountain" story:

   When the girl climbed up the mountain, she saw, hidden among the trees, a little wooden house covered in snow.

Overall, there were 54 stories per group, totaling 162 stories in the corpus. This corpus is particularly well suited to analyse difficulties with cohesion because it contains texts that were freely invented, without any structural guidance. Moreover, the inclusion of the language-matched and the age-matched control groups enables us to distinguish language development issues from ASD-specific difficulties.

3.2 Corpus annotations and statistics

The stories were recorded, transcribed and manually coded and scored according to the Narrative Scoring Scheme (Stein and Albro, 1997, NSS). The NSS rates stories on a 0-5 scale in several categories: introduction, character development, mental states, referencing, conflict/resolution, cohesion and conclusion. To ensure the reliability of the coding, 10% of the narratives (16) were also coded by an independent researcher. Inter-reliability was found to be high (0.87).

Because we are specifically interested in discourse structure, the NSS annotations for cohesion will serve as a gold standard for our own evaluation (cf. Section 5.2). We show these ratings along with some basic corpus figures in Table 1:

Cohesion refers to the manual cohesion annotations, *Sent. / Story* is the average number of utterances per story, and *Words / Sent.* quantifies the average number of words per sentence.

The ASD group has significantly lower cohesion scores than the two comparison groups (*Lang.* for the group matched by language competence, *Age* for the controls matched by chronological age). Between the two groups with neurotypical participants, there is no significant difference. The *mountain* story prompt resulted in longer, more cohesive stories, consisting of shorter sentences. This difference is particularly clear for the ASD group and the age-matched controls.

4 Measures for Story Cohesion

In a preprocessing step, we apply the coreference resolution module of Stanford CoreNLP (Manning et al., 2014) to the whole corpus. On this basis, we compute three coreference-related measures: the proportion of sentences with anaphoric references, the average length of coreference chains (normalized by story length) and *Skewness*, a measure we derive from statistics and apply to clusterings.

4.1 Sentences with anaphoric references

As a simple measure for cohesion in a text t, we define $anaphors(t)$ as the proportion of sentences that contain at least one anaphoric reference (with $sentences(t)$ being the set of sentences in t):

$$anaphors(t) = \frac{|(sentences\ w.\ anaphors\ in\ t)|}{|sentences(t)|}$$

4.2 Average length of coreference chains

The average length of coreference chains in a text is a common indicator for cohesion (the longer the chains, the stronger the cohesion). Computing this as an absolute number will also directly measure the average text length, which is always lower for the ASD group. In order to isolate the cohesion part, we divide the average coreference chain length by the number of sentences in the text. We compute $chain\_length(t)$ of a text t as follows (with C_t as the set of all coreference chains in t):

$$chain\_length(t) = \frac{\sum\limits_{c \in C_t} length(C)}{|C_t| * |sentences(t)|}$$

The average chain length for the same story will be higher if there are fewer coreference sets (and thus fewer characters and objects).

4.3 *Skewness* of coreference chains

As a third coherence measure, we introduce the notion of *Skewness* for coreference chains. Skewness is originally a measure for probability distributions, indicating (the lack of) uniformity.

We interpret this score as a geometric measure for a set partition: for mentions in different coreference chains, this measure shows whether the narrator has the tendency to devote equally long story parts to all participants (resembling a uniform distribution) or whether he or she focuses more on a few main characters or objects, with some supporting entities which are less frequently mentioned (skewed distribution). We thus interpret the distribution of mentions as a probability distribution Pr over a random variable x, with each value x_i in X corresponding to a coreference chain c_i in $C(t)$, and $Pr(X = x_i)$ being the number of mentions in c_i divided by the overall number of mentions. $skewness(t)$ is computed as follows (with E being the expectation operator, μ the mean of the distribution X, σ the standard deviation):

$$skewness(t) = abs\left(\mathbf{E}\left[\left(\frac{X - \mu}{\sigma}\right)^3\right]\right)$$

Skewness originally does not only indicate the strength, but also the *direction* using negative or positive values. Because we are only interested in the overall asymmetry of the coreference chains, we only note the absolute value of the result. According to Bulmer (1979), a result with an absolute value greater than 1 is considered to indicate strong skewness.

4.4 Measure combinations

In the final evaluation, we also use pairwise measure combinations, and the combination of all three together. *Combining* here means that we first make the measures comparable, and then average the results. To arrive at meaningful scores, we process the chain length and skewness as follows:

- The **coreference chain length** correlates negatively with human judgements (cf. Table 3), so we combine a "negative chain length" ($1 - chain\_length$) with the respective other measure.

- **Skewness** is normalized to a value between 0 and 1 before combination to match the value span of the other two measures.

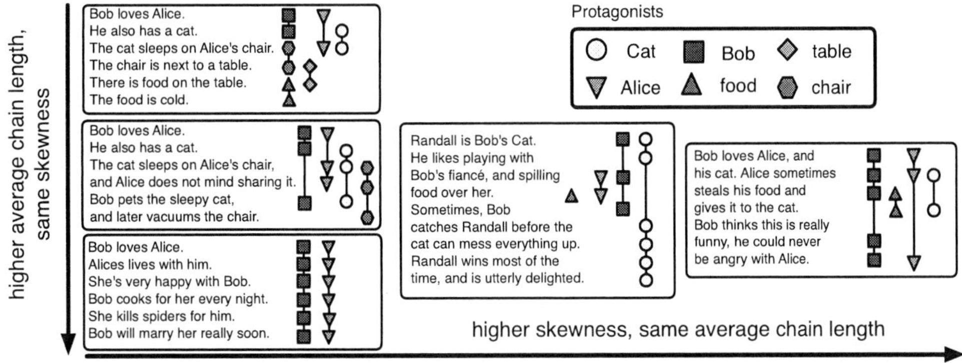

Figure 1: Constructed examples illustrating chain length vs. skewness

To better illustrate the relationship of skewness and chain length, Figure 1 shows examplary (made-up) stories with coreference chains of different lengths and skewness. The left column shows three stories with the same skewness (0), but different average chain length (2, 4 and 6, top to bottom, without normalization). An inverse case is sketched in the middle row: the chains all have the same average chain length (4), but different skewness (0,1.2 and1.4 respectively). Despite the equally trivial plots, the stories with 4 or more characters appear more readable when their coreference clusters are more skewed.

5 Experiments

In the following, we first compare the ASD group with the two control groups using our cohesion measures and their combinations (Section 5.1).

In a second step, we show the correlation of our measures with human coherence annotations reported by King et al. (2014) (Section 5.2).

5.1 Comparison of the three groups

The computed results for all measures and their combination is shown in Table 2.

Viewed in isolation, only the number of sentences with anaphors distinguishes the ASD group from the two control groups. While the (normalized) average coreference chain length is equal for all groups, skewness seems to be a matter of language competence rather than exposing anomalies from the ASD group. However, the picture is not entirely clear: when just considering the "forest" stories, we see a tendency for the ASD group to have less skewed coreference chains.

The combination of anaphoric references plus the average chain length distinguishes the ASD group most clearly, showing no difference between the two neurotypical groups (even though they differ in general language competence). The same pattern is evident in the expert annotation with NSS scores: there is no difference between the control groups, but the stories from the ASD group are rated significantly as less cohesive.

All other combinations distinguish all three groups from each other, which means that the differences between the groups are related to both ASD and language competence. For the combination of anaphoric references with skewness, our data indicates that the group differences are more strongly related to factors specific to ASD: the alpha level for the significance of the difference between the two control groups is lower than for the remaining differences ($p < 0.05$, whereas all other significance levels are at $p < 0.01$).

The remaining two feature combinations (chain length with skewness, all three measures together) also distinguish the ASD group from the comparison groups, but (as expected) additionally bear components of language competency.

5.2 Correlation with manual annotations

The results of our automated evaluation were mixed with respect to ability to distinguish the ASD group from the comparison groups. From the isolated measures, only counting sentences with anaphoric references shows results specific for the ASD group. The combinations of different cohesion components gives a clearer picture, but only one combination shows the same pattern observed for manual annotations: the neurotypical groups are indistinguishable for the combination of anaphors and chain length.

To understand better what contributes most to

Measure	FOREST			MOUNTAIN			ALL STORIES		
	ASD	Lang	Age	ASD	Lang	Age	ASD	Lang	Age
anaphors (an)	0.83	0.93	0.95	0.80	0.92	0.91	0.81	0.93	0.93*
chain length (cl)	0.56	0.52	0.55	0.47	0.47	0.44	0.51*	*0.50*	*0.50**
skewness (skew)	0.79	0.91	1.04	0.95	0.97	1.22	0.90*	*1.04*	1.30*
an & cl	0.73	0.80	0.80	0.75	0.81	0.81	0.74	0.80	0.81*
an & skew	0.54	0.63	0.66	0.56	0.62	0.68	0.55	0.63	0.67
cl & skew	0.35	0.41	0.41	0.42	0.43	0.50	0.39	0.42	0.46
All Combined	0.57	0.64	0.66	0.61	0.65	0.69	0.59	0.65	0.67
NSS score	1.79	2.93	2.76	2.21	2.96	3.04	2.00	2.95	*2.90*

Table 2: Results of cohesion evaluation, along with the manually assigned cohesion scores. Significance is measured for the group of all stories only. *Emphasized* values have no significant difference (p > 0.05) to the ASD group, starred values * have no significant difference to the language-matched group.

the cohesion perceptions of human experts, we calculate the correlation of our measures with the NSS scores assigned in our source dataset. To measure correlation, we use Spearman's rank correlation coefficient (ρ), a non-parametric test which is widely used for similar comparisons of system ratings with manually assigned scores (Mitchell and Lapata, 2008; Erk and McCarthy, 2009, among others). Spearman's ρ compares how similarly two measures rank the same set of samples (in our case, a sample is a story).

Table 3 shows the results. For the complete corpus, all measures show significant correlations.

The best isolated measure is skewness ($\rho = 0.44$), which shows the highest correlation for the mountain stories. However, combining skewness with any of the other measures does not result in a higher ρ value. A partial explanation lies in the differences in story length: We did not normalize skewness for story length, because "skewness per sentence" is not a meaningful measure. However, skewness of coreference chains is intuitively a more distinguishing feature if the stories are longer, simply because the possible skewness values have a higher range when there are more referring elements to distribute. In contrast, the other measures seem to be less suitable for longer texts, because skewness has the highest ρ values on the *mountain* stories, which are, on average, longer than the *forest* stories.

The average chain length has a significant negative correlation, i.e. cohesion is higher when the chains are shorter on average. (For combinations, we therefore use an inverted value, cf. Section 4).

Measure	FOREST	MOUNTAIN	ALL
anaphors (an)	0.23	0.17	0.19
chain length (cl)	-0.31	-0.22	-0.28
skewness (skew)	0.48	**0.38**	0.44
an & cl	0.55	0.36	**0.46**
an & skew	0.54	0.09 (ns)	0.31
cl & skew	0.47	0.13 (ns)	0.31
All Combined	**0.57**	0.21	0.40

Table 3: Correlation with manual evaluation (in Spearman's ρ). Values in italics are *not significant* (p > 0.05), **maxima** are in boldface.

The number of anaphoric references displays the lowest ρ-values (for the *mountain* sub-corpus, the correlation is not significant). When combined with coreference chain length, the fused measure has the highest overall correlation ($\rho = 0.46$), so these two features make different contributions to the overall cohesion.

The combination of all three measures has the second highest correlation with the manual annotations, and the highest ρ for the forest prompt.

Overall, our automated measures correlate strongly with the human annotations, but surprisingly much more so for the forest stories compared to the mountain stories. Skewness seems to be a very good measure in general, but the number of reference-bearing sentences combined with the average chain length obviously contributes similar information to the evaluation of short stories.

6 Discussion

The measures we evaluated are all coreference-based, quantifying different aspects of text cohesion: the proportion of sentences with anaphoric references reflects the sheer number of coreference links. The average coreference chain length (normalized over story length) mainly measures the number of protagonists and objects (cf. Figure 1). Skewness applied to coreference sets shows whether the protagonists differ in importance within the story, i.e. whether there is a recognizable main character (or a few of them) next to several supporting characters (or objects).

We succeeded in demonstrating that these measures strongly correlate with human assessment of cohesion, and that some combinations of them yield different results for the stories from the ASD group compared to the control groups. In particular, the measure combination that showed the strongest correlation with human judgements (chain length plus number of anaphoric references) seems to be directly influenced by ASD, and not just an indicator of general language competence: there was no difference between the two neurotypical control groups, but the score of the ASD group differed significantly from both.

Skewness, which we used as a new measure for quantifying the distribution of referring expressions into coreference sets, shows the highest correlation with human judgement as an isolated measure. However, skewness seems to work better for longer stories, which is intuitively clear: the possible variation of coreference set distribution is higher if there are more anaphoric references, and skewness becomes more distinguishing if the results show a higher variation.

Obviously, our measures cannot assess the whole spectrum of discourse features: they do not include any lexical features or semantic discourse relations. While we tried to compute such indicators, neither lexical chains nor discourse relations lead to a meaningful evaluation on our dataset. This is mostly due to the brevity of the stories, but is also because the setup of oral narration does not yield the discourse structure typically found in written language. Analyses with deeper discourse features would require a different dataset, which, however, might be difficult to create.

The most important outcome of this analysis is that an automatic evaluation of cohesion for diagnostic stylometry can be successfully used to validate theoretical claims. We also took important steps towards identifying cohesion-based measures to analyze unusual language traits in adolescents with autistic spectrum disorder. Our measures proved suitable for short stories, which is important because the participants we focus on have difficulties with producing longer texts. Further, our approach is robust enough to assess cohesion in transcripts of spoken narrations, which are more difficult to process with than written language. Future work needs to show how our ideas can be extended beyond this point, either with different measures, or with different datasets, or both.

7 Conclusion

We have presented an automatic evaluation showing differences in stories narrated by adolescents with autistic spectrum disorder in comparison with two control groups. For this purpose, we presented three robust measures applicable to the short story transcripts, namely the proportion of sentences with anaphors, the (normalized) average coreference chain length, and skewness as a new measure related to coreference set clusterings.

We showed that skewness is the measure that best correlates with manual cohesion annotation, and that it seems to be more meaningful for longer stories. Further we have shown that the combination of coreference chain length and the number of sentences with anaphors is sufficient to assess cohesion in shorter stories.

In future work, we would seek to find other measures of cohesion which could help to assess the difficulties of individuals with ASD compared to neurotypical controls, possibly on a different dataset with longer stories. Further, it would be interesting to establish whether the features that we found persist with age, and whether they are comparable to the effects reported for other disorders and diseases such as dementia.

References

American Psychiatric Association. 2013. *Diagnostic and statistical manual of mental disorders: DSM-5*. APA, Washington, DC, 5th ed. edition.

Vassilis Baldas, Charalampos Lampiris, Christos Capsalis, and Dimitrios Koutsouris. 2011. Early Diagnosis of Alzheimer's Type Dementia Using Continuous Speech Recognition. In *Lecture Notes of the Institute for Computer Sciences, Social Informatics and Telecommunications Engineering*. Springer Berlin Heidelberg.

M.G. Bulmer. 1979. *Principles of Statistics*. Dover Books on Mathematics Series. Dover Publications.

Lisa Capps, Molly Losh, and Christopher Thurber. 2000. "The Frog Ate the Bug and Made his Mouth Sad": Narrative Competence in Children with Autism. *Journal of Abnormal Child Psychology*, 28(2).

Walter Daelemans. 2013. Explanation in computational stylometry. In *Proc. of CICLing'13*.

Joshua J. Diehl, Loisa Bennetto, and Edna Carter Young. 2006. Story Recall and Narrative Coherence of High-Functioning Children with Autism Spectrum Disorders. *Journal of Abnormal Child Psychology*, 34(1).

Lloyd M. Dunn and Leota M. Dunn. 1997. *The British Picture Vocabulary Scale Second Edition (BPVS II)*. Windsor Berkshire: NFER-NELSON Publication Company.

Colin Elliot, Pauline Smith, and Kay McCullouch. 1996. *The British Ability Scales II (BASII)*. Windsor Berkshire: NFER-NELSON Publication Company.

Katrin Erk and Diana McCarthy. 2009. Graded word sense assignment. In *Proc. of EMNLP 2009*.

Keyur Gabani, Melissa Sherman, Thamar Solorio, Yang Liu, Lisa Bedore, and Elizabeth Peña. 2009. A corpus-based approach for the prediction of language impairment in monolingual english and spanish-english bilingual children. In *Proc. of NAACL-HLT 2009*.

Graeme Hirst and Vanessa Wei Feng. 2012. Changes in style in authors with alzheimer's disease. *English Studies*, 93(3).

Kai Hong, Christian G. Kohler, Mary E. March, Amber A. Parker, and Ani Nenkova. 2012. Lexical differences in autobiographical narratives from schizophrenic patients and healthy controls. In *Proc. of EMNLP-CoNLL 2012*.

Annette Karmiloff-Smith. 1985. Language and cognitive processes from a developmental perspective. *Language and Cognitive Processes*, 1(1).

Diane King, Julie Dockrell, and Morag Stuart. 2014. Constructing fictional stories: a study of story narratives by children with autistic spectrum disorder. *Research in developmental disabilities*, 35(10).

Xuan Le, Ian Lancashire, Graeme Hirst, and Regina Jokel. 2011. Longitudinal detection of dementia through lexical and syntactic changes in writing: a case study of three british novelists. *Literary and Linguistic Computing*, 26(4).

Katherine Loveland and Belgin Tunali. 1993. Narrative language in autism and the theory of mind hypothesis: a wider perspective. In *Understanding other minds: Perspectives from autism*. Oxford University Press.

Hans Peter Luhn. 1957. A statistical approach to mechanized encoding and searching of literary information. *IBM J. Res. Dev.*, 1(4).

Christopher D. Manning, Mihai Surdeanu, John Bauer, Jenny Finkel, Steven J. Bethard, and David Mc-Closky. 2014. The Stanford CoreNLP natural language processing toolkit. In *Proc. of ACL 2014: System Demonstrations*.

Jeff Mitchell and Mirella Lapata. 2008. Vector-based models of semantic composition. In *Proc. of ACL 2008*.

Emily T Prud'hommeaux, Brian Roark, Lois M Black, and Jan van Santen. 2011. Classification of atypical language in autism. *ACL HLT 2011*.

Michaela Regneri and Diane King. 2015. Automatically evaluating atypical language in narratives by children with autistic spectrum disorder. In *Proc. of NLPCS 2014*.

Kathryn P. Riley, David A. Snowdon, Mark F. Desrosiers, and William R. Markesbery. 2005. Early life linguistic ability, late life cognitive function, and neuropathology: findings from the Nun Study. *Neurobiology of Aging*, 26(3).

Brian Roark, Margaret Mitchell, J Hosom, Kristy Hollingshead, and Jeffrey Kaye. 2011. Spoken language derived measures for detecting mild cognitive impairment. *Audio, Speech, and Language Processing, IEEE Transactions on*, 19(7).

Masoud Rouhizadeh, Emily Prud'hommeaux, Brian Roark, and Jan van Santen. 2013. Distributional semantic models for the evaluation of disordered language. In *Proc. of NAACL-HLT 2013*.

Masoud Rouhizadeh, Emily Prud'Hommeaux, Jan Van Santen, and Richard Sproat. 2015. Measuring idiosyncratic interests in children with autism. In *Proc. of ACL 2015*.

Eleanor Semel, Elisabeth .H Wiig, and Wayne Secord. 2006. *Clinical Evaluation of Language Fundamentals (CELF-4 UK)*. Pearson Assessment, fourth edition uk edition.

Nancy L Stein and Elizabeth R Albro. 1997. Building complexity and coherence: Children's use of of goal-structured knowledge in telling stories. *Narrative development: Six approaches*, page 5.

Helen Tager-Flusberg and Kate Sullivan. 1995. Attributing mental states to story characters: A comparison of narratives produced by autistic and mentally retarded individuals. *Applied Psycholinguistics*, 16.

Helen Tager-Flusberg. 1996. Brief report: Current theory and research on language and communication in autism. *Journal of Autism and Developmental Disorders*, 26(2).

Appendix A   Corpus Examples

The following shows some examples from our story corpus collected by King et al. (2014). For each story stem (repeated below), we show 2 examples from the ASD group, and one from each control group. For the sake of brevity, we do not show the manual annotations from the original corpus. Slashes (/) indicate utterance boundaries.

A.1   The *Forest* story

The boy ran into the forest. He looked ahead of him and saw a little green man in a spaceship.

A.1.1   ASD

Example 1: the spaceship was quite small. / And the alien was about the size of a small cat. / And it was friendly. / but it didn't really understand how humans said hello. / So it thought, to say 'hello' you had to vaporise the person in front of you. / and then the boy ran away, shut his door and then decided not to drink anymore whisky or beer.

Example 2: The green man had three eyes. / It had claws and fangs. / It looked at him and ran into the spaceship. / Out came three more green men carrying laser guns, dun dun dun.

A.1.2   Language-Matched Controls

He was shocked at first because he didn't know what it is. / So he walked up. / and he got suck/ed in by a tractor beam. / and he found himself in a UFO. / he was surround/ed by weird looking creatures like aliens. / and they started speaking like this unknown language to him. / and he couldn't understand a thing about them. / So he tried to escape. / he ran away. / but he couldn't cos—because wherever he went he was surround/ed by aliens. / and they eventually capture/ed him and took him off to Mars. /

A.1.3   Age-Matched Controls

The little green man waved at him and yelled at him to come and help him with his spaceship which had crashed into the forest after he had lost all his fuel. / The little boy went up to him and said that he didn't know what much he could do because he's obviously not very talented at fixing alien space craft. / so he ran out of the forest went to go get the nearest person he could see. / He then brought him back to the spaceship where the little green man was waiting. / and the man he'd brought back was absolutely amazed. / he went up to the little alien and started speaking with him. / And then after a while he persuaded it to come out of it's spaceship. / and it went to meet the locals who were very very amazed. / and then all the people joined together. / and they pulled his spaceship out of the mud. / and he flew back in it to mars.

A.2   The *Mountain* story

When the girl climbed up the mountain, she saw, hidden among the trees, a little wooden house covered in snow.

A.2.1   ASD

Example 1: She went up to the mountain to see the house. / She went inside and had a cup of tea. / After that she can't get out because the snow block/ed the door. / And the men came came in and broke it. / but snow came again. / and then she was stuck. / That's it.

Example 2: the snow house was was a zombie. / and the zombie / he went up to the door. / and the zombie scared him. / and the zombie went to chase the girl. / and the girl ran away to to her grandma that was climbing up the mountain. / and she screamed and jumped off the mountain

A.2.2   Language-Matched Controls

She saw it was abandoned. / so she went down to see what it was like. / She peeked inside the window. / and inside there was a pixie . / and then the pixie saw the girl and said 'go away from my window'. / and then he threw a bowl of soup over her. / the little girl went home and said: 'daddy there was a pixie who threw some soup over me'. / and then the dad said 'don't be silly'. / stop telling your little stories'.

A.2.3   Age-Matched Controls

She walked towards the house. / the house lit up. / lights switched on. / She knocked on the door. / she was cold. / she asked if she could come in. / There was a strange lady come to the door, pimples and spots all over her, mouldy ugly hair and very very small. / she went in. / the lady was actually a witch in disguise. / She grabbed the girl and threw her into the oven. / her friend had also came into the house five minutes later and seen her in the oven. / She had pushed the witch over, got her out and ran off. / they reported it all to the police. / The police came up the next day. / The house was not there.

Detection of Alzheimer's disease based on automatic analysis of common objects descriptions

Laura Hernández-Domínguez
ÉTS, Quebec University
1100 Notre-Dame
Montreal, QC H3C1K3
laudobla
@gmail.com

Edgar García-Cano
ÉTS, Quebec Univ.
1100 Notre-Dame
Montreal, H3C1K3
eegkno
@gmail.com

Sylvie Ratté
ÉTS, Quebec Univ.
1100 Notre-Dame
Montreal, H3C1K3
Sylvie.Ratte
@etsmtl.ca

Gerardo Sierra-Martínez
IINGEN, UNAM
Ciudad Universitaria
Mexico City, 04510
GSierraM
@iingen.unam.mx

Abstract

Many studies have been made on the language alterations that take place over the course of Alzheimer's disease (AD). As a consequence, it is now admitted that it is possible to discriminate between healthy and ailing patients solely based on the analysis of language production. Most of these studies, however, were made on very small samples—30 participants per study, on an average—, or involved a great deal of manual work in their analysis. In this paper, we present an automatic analysis of transcripts of elderly participants describing six common objects. We used part-of-speech and lexical richness as linguistic features to train an SVM classifier to automatically discriminate between healthy and AD patients in the early and moderate stages. The participants, in the corpus used for this study, were 63 Spanish adults over 55 years old (29 controls and 34 AD patients). With an accuracy of 88%, our experimental results compare favorably to those relying on the manual extraction of attributes, providing evidence that the need for manual analysis can be overcome without sacrificing in performance.

1 Introduction

As life expectancy increases, age-related disorders increase as well, bringing great social, health and economic challenges for governments and societies in general. Researchers across the world are trying to find methods for detecting and treating these disorders in effective, non-invasive and cost-efficient ways.

AD affects one in ten adults over 65 years old in the United States (Alzheimer's Association, 2015). Interventions may be more effective in the early stages of dementia. Nevertheless, it is highly common, especially in low and middle income countries, to diagnose AD several years after the disease begins, leading to a treatment gap for early dementia sufferers (Alzheimer's Disease International, 2011). This gap could reduce the effectiveness of treatments, prolonging the patients' state of reduced independence. Alzheimer's Disease International (2015) identifies early diagnosis and treatment as a means of attenuating care costs and reducing this gap. Furthermore, an early diagnosis would allow the sufferers and their families to get their affairs in order by foreseeing the future better and preparing accordingly.

Many researchers have studied the early detection of AD. These studies usually follow two main approaches: the analysis of biomarkers and the examination of patients' decreasing cognitive abilities. The first approach yields reliable results in the detection of AD in its moderate and advanced stages, albeit still performing insufficiently in the early stages of the disease (Alzheimer's Association, 2015). The second approach has gained more attention in recent years, due to the fact that, in clinical practice, it has shown promise in the early detection of AD (Taler and Phillips, 2008; Schröder et al., 2010). Furthermore, when compared to the first approach, the analysis of the decline of cognitive abilities represents an inexpensive and noninvasive alternative.

Language skills are among the first cognitive abilities to diminish during the course of AD, with alterations appearing even before any symptom is experienced. Clinicians have designed many standard tests to evaluate language in elderly patients (Taler and Phillips, 2008), such as asking them to retrieve words from certain categories, to think of words that start with the same letter, to

Proceedings of the 7th Workshop on Cognitive Aspects of Computational Language Learning, pages 10–15,
Berlin, Germany, August 11, 2016. ©2016 Association for Computational Linguistics

name objects in pictures, etc. These tests, although sufficient to give a reasonably accurate diagnosis, present some problems in the clinical practice (Smith and Bondi, 2013). Such problems include production of nervousness and discomfort in elderly patients, as well as a "practice effect". Also, these tests do not necessarily describe patients' real performance in language production. This, apart from aiding in early detection of the disease, could help further our understanding of the disease, its progression and the parts of the brain affected in early stages (before the damage can be visible on MRI images).

In this article, we introduce our first experimental approach for automatic analysis of transcripts from elderly Spanish speakers. We aim to discriminate cognitively-healthy participants from (early and moderate) AD sufferers.

2 Related Work

Relatively few authors (Bucks et al., 2000; Jarrold et al., 2010; Guinn and Habash, 2012; Guinn et al., 2014; Jarrold et al., 2014; Alegria et al., 2013) have researched the automatic discrimination of AD patients using language analyses of transcripts, although there is a growing interest in recent years. In most studies, researchers examined the free discourse of elderly English-speakers. The most often-used features are part-of-speech rates, lexical richness measures, pauses, and incomplete words. Overall accuracy ranges from 73% to 95%, but between authors there is a disagreement on the features used. Some works, like Khodabakhsh et al. (2015) even minimize the usefulness of these types of features.

Most of these studies used very small samples (8-32 AD patients and 16-51 controls) taken in different settings (phone/face-to-face conversations, hospital/familiar environment, inconsistent thematics, etc.). These differences make it difficult comparing their findings. Given the small size of the samples, it would be helpful to use corpora with constrained settings, like restricted discourse and controlled environments, in order to discard differences attributable to factors unrelated to language. Moreover, further studies with non-English speakers would help us to enrich our understanding of language alterations due to AD.

In a different approach, Guerrero et al. (2016) trained a Bayesian Network using manually extracted conceptual components along with age, gender, and educational level as prior probabilities to detect AD. Their corpus consisted of transcripts of Spanish elderly participants orally describing six objects (Peraita and Grasso, 2010). The authors reported the following performance—accuracy, precision, recall (sensitivity), F_1-score, false positive rate, and false negative rate—:

Acc	Pre	Rec	F_1	FPR	FNR
0.91	0.94	0.87	0.90	0.05	0.01

Table 1: Results by Guerrero et al. (2015).

For this work, we studied the restricted-discourse corpus used in Guerrero et al. (2016), and trained an SVM using some of the linguistic features used by previous authors in the analysis of free conversations. We additionally incorporated two scarcely explored part-of-speech-based features—*conjunction rate* and *secondary verb rate*—. We compared our automatic analysis results to those obtained by Guerrero et al. using manually extracted conceptual components.

3 Methods

3.1 Corpus

Peraita and Grasso (2010) created a dataset[1] of oral descriptions in Spanish to study linguistic pathologies related to dementia, particularly AD. All recollections were obtained with the written informed consent of the participants (Grasso et al., 2011). The authors granted us permission to use their corpus for this study. We choose this corpus because its availability, restricted discourse and homogeneous recollections facilitate the comparison of our results with those of other researchers. Likewise, the size of this sample is comparable to the largest samples used in related works.

The cohort used by Guerrero et al. (2016) in their study includes a total of 69 participants (30 controls and 39 AD patients previously diagnosed by neurologists) aged between 55 and 95 years old. For each participant, Peraita and Grasso recorded free oral descriptions of six common objects (referred in their work as "semantic categories"): *dog*, *apple*, *pine* (living things), *car*, *trousers* and *chair* (non-living things). These descriptions were manually transcribed. Any interactions with or interventions by the interviewer

---

[1]http://www.uned.es/investigacion-corpuslinguistico/

> **Participant's description of *dog***:
>
> *"It is a loving animal. They are loving. They love the owner. They obey him. You leave him home alone and he cries. He misses you and when you arrive home he is very glad to see you. He guards the house pretty well. When he hears a noise in the stairs, he barks, meaning, he guards the house. They like you to pet them, to love them. They make great company."*
>
> **Conceptual components**:
> *Taxonomic*:
> - it's an animal.
> *Functional*:
> - he guards the house;
> - they make great company.
> *Evaluative*:
> - they are loving; [...]

Figure 1: Translated sample from the corpus.

were excluded from the transcription. In addition, the authors of the corpus noted if a participant went "off-topic", but did not include these utterances in the transcript. They annotated this corpus to show marks of interruptions, off-topic, and unintelligible words.

In their study, Peraita and Grasso (2010) manually analyzed and extracted attributes from the description of each object. These attributes were divided into eleven categories: *taxonomic, types, parts, functional, evaluative, places/habitat, behavior, cause/generate, procedural, life cycle,* and *others*. In Figure 1, we provide a translated version of a sample taken from the corpus.

From the sample, we removed all participants with no utterances in the description of one or more objects. Additionally, since our objective was to evaluate the performance of a classifier for early detection of AD, we proceeded like Guerrero et al. (2016) and only considered the controls and patients in the early and moderate stages of AD. Our final sample consisted of a total of 63 participants (29 controls and 34 AD patients).

3.2 Linguistic features

For this work, we used a combination of 5 features that most authors have found suitable: verb, noun and preposition rates, Brunet's W index, and Honoré's R Statistics. Additionally, in a previous non-automatic study regarding the preservation of syntax in AD, Kemper et al. (1993) found

that sentences produced by cognitively healthy adults usually contain more secondary verbs and conjunctions. We incorporated these findings, resulting in a total of 7 features.

Part-Of-Speech features:

- *Verb, noun, preposition* and ***conjunction rates***: the number of verbs, nouns, prepositions and conjunctions per 100 words, respectively.

- ***Secondary verb rate***: number of secondary verbs divided by the total number of verbs.

Lexical richness features:

- We used *Brunet's W index* (Brunet, 1978) to determine the richness of speakers' vocabularies:

$$W = N^{(V-1.165)} \qquad (1)$$

Where N is the total number of words used and V is the vocabulary size (number of different words used).

- *Honoré's R Statistics* (Honoré, 1979) measures lexical richness based on the number of a speakers once-mentioned words:

$$R = (100 log N)/(1 - V_1/V) \qquad (2)$$

Where N is the total number of words used, V is the vocabulary size, and V_1 is the number of words mentioned only once.

3.3 Implementation

To perform the binary classification, we used a Support Vector Machine (SVM) implementation of the Python library scikit-learn (Pedregosa et al., 2011). For the automatic tokenization, lemmatization, and part-of-speech extraction, we used FreeLing 3.0 (Padró and Stanilovsky, 2012), an open source language analysis tool suite. We selected this package for its good performance in Spanish (although it also supports other languages), and for the way it encapsulates multiple text analysis services in a single application.

In their experiments, Guerrero et al. (2016) trained their Bayesian Network without directly linking risk factor variables (such as age, gender, or education) to the rest of the model. Instead, they used these *a priori* probabilities as deterministic inputs. In our experiments, we did not consider these variables. We performed our classification based solely on linguistic features.

Using the above-mentioned risk factor variables and their correlation to AD could be useful in the improvement of the overall accuracy of these types of experiments. However, these correlations vary significantly depending on factors such as country, race, quality of life, diet, pollution, environment, etc. Moreover, in most countries, there are no reliable statistics about these correlations (Alzheimer's Disease International, 2015). Furthermore, most AD datasets have very few participants, and their distributions are not usually an accurate representation of the population. In practice, training an algorithm with the socio-demographic information presented in these datasets would lead to biased results.

In the core of their Bayesian Network, Guerrero et al. (2016) calculated the probability of a person having a lexical-semantic-conceptual deficit (LSCD)—which is considered by the authors as a major sign of cognitive impairment—in two main categories: "living things" and "non-living things". The authors obtained these probabilities based on the number of attributes present on each of the 11 categories; first individually for each object, and then jointly for the main category to which they belonged (living / non-living things). The reason behind this categorical division is that previous researchers have found an important difference in the number of attributes of living and non-living things in the descriptions given by AD patients in early stages and those given by healthy individuals. The authors used the k-means++ algorithm to discretize the presence of LSCD given the number of living and non-living things' attributes mentioned by a participant.

We designed two different experiments. In the first experiment, we followed the lead of Guerrero et al. (2016) and divided each human subject's descriptions into living and non-living things. From this, we extracted a total of 14 linguistic features (*set1*): 7 features (verb, noun, preposition, secondary verb and conjunction rates, Brunet's *W* index, and Honoré's *R* Statistics) from their descriptions of living things, and (the same) 7 features from their descriptions of non-living things. In the second experiment, we considered all the descriptions from each human subject as a unit and extracted the 7 linguistic features (*set2*).

Calibration: We tested two SVM kernels for

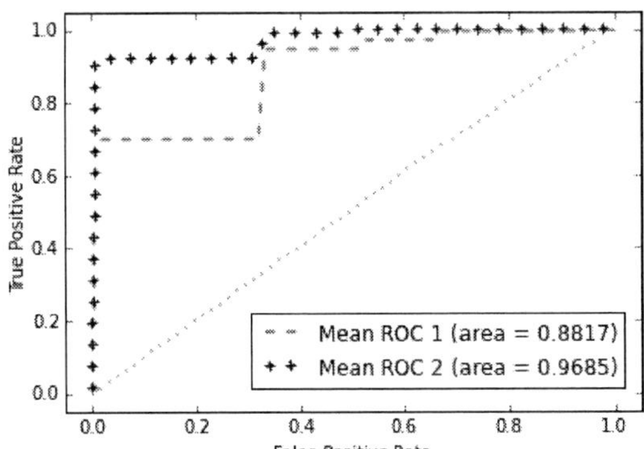

Figure 2: ROC curves and areas under the curves for the classifiers trained with *set1* and *set2*.

both experiments, linear and Radial Basis Function (RBF). We used a 5-fold cross validation to calibrate the value of their respective hyperparameters. Cross validation used 80% of the data for training and 20% for testing. We shuffled the training and testing samples and selected them at random. For *set1*, the best model (**accuracy=86%**) used an RBF kernel (C=1.0, gamma=0.0001). The best model (**accuracy=88%**) for *set2* used a linear kernel (C=0.1). The best models' accuracies reflect the performance of the classifiers when dealing with completely unseen data.

4 Results

We evaluated the two best models using 5-times-10-fold cross-validation over the dataset. In Table 2 we show the average of the most common performance metrics—accuracy, precision, recall (sensitivity), F_1-score, FPR (false positive rate), and FNR (false negative rate)—used for medical applications. Additionally, we obtained the ROC curves and areas under the curves (AUC) for both experiments (see Figure 2).

Set	Acc	Pre	Rec	F_1	FPR	FNR
1	0.87	**0.91**	0.88	0.88	**0.08**	0.12
2	**0.88**	0.89	**0.90**	0.88	0.10	**0.10**

Table 2: Performance metrics obtained with the classifier trained with *set1* and *set2*.

5 Discussion and future directions

As shown in Table 2, the differences in accuracy and F_1-score between the AD classifiers trained with *set1* and *set2* of features are not very perceptible. The classifier of the second experiment has a slightly higher sensitivity (2% more), which means that it has a lower tendency of letting AD participants go unrecognized. When comparing the AUC of both classifiers, the difference is more noticeable; *set2* performed better than *set1*. From this, we concluded that for the linguistic features considered, there is no need to separate participants' descriptions into living and non-living categories.

Guerrero et al. (2016) reported an accuracy of 91% (see Table 1) and an AUC of 0.9636. They used a Bayesian Network fed with manually-extracted attributes and incorporated participants' socio-demographic information as *a priori* deterministic inputs. We obtained an accuracy of 88% and an AUC of 0.9685 by performing automatic language analysis, without taking into account any socio-demographic information. Although the manually extracted attributes' classifier performs slightly better, automatic language analysis reduces time and human effort and provides consistency and replicability.

There is another cohort of 143 speakers from Argentina in the corpus used in this work. The corpus is provided in a read-only application, and manually transforming the data into text format took a great amount of time. For this reason, we only analyzed the cohort of Spanish participants as Guerrero et al. (2016) did. To our knowledge, no experimental work has been done over it yet. Our next step will be to experiment with this cohort to explore intralanguage variations. We also intend to perform a study on less restrictive discourse contexts, like the work of Prud'hommeaux and Roark (2011) with story retellings.

For our first set of experiments, we selected some basic linguistic features commonly used in free spontaneous discourse analysis, but applied them to a particular restricted discourse context with very encouraging results for detecting AD in its early and moderate stages. In future experiments we will test more sophisticated linguistic features, and perform computational syntactic and semantic analysis. Furthermore, we will investigate performance of other classification algorithms. An in-depth analysis of features used and their relevance in this task is also planned.

Acknowledgments

We would like to thank Prof. Herminia Peraita from the National University of Distance Education in Spain for sharing her dataset. This research was partially supported by the FRQNT 177601 and 194703 files, the CONACYT 323619 scholarship, and the Ministère des Relations Internationales et de la Francophonie and CONACYT Mexico (XV Groupe de Travail Québec-Mexique 2015-2017).

References

Renne Alegria, Celia Gallo, Mirian Bolso, Bernardo dos Santos, Cleide Rosana Prisco, Cassio Bottino, and Nogueira Maria Ines. 2013. Comparative study of the uses of grammatical categories: Adjectives, adverbs, pronouns, interjections, conjunctions and prepositions in patients with Alzheimer's disease. *Alzheimer's & dementia: the journal of the Alzheimer's Association*, 9(4):P882, jul.

Alzheimer's Association. 2015. 2015 Alzheimer's Disease Facts and Figures. Technical report, Alzheimer's Association.

Alzheimer's Disease International. 2011. World Alzheimer Report 2011. The benefits of early diagnosis and intervention. Technical report, Alzheimer's Disease International.

Alzheimer's Disease International. 2015. World Alzheimer Report 2015. The Global Impact of Dementia. Technical report, Alzheimer's Disease International.

Etienne Brunet. 1978. *Vocabulaire de Jean Giraudoux: structure et évolution: statistique et informatique appliquées à l'étude des textes à partir des données du Trésor de la langue*. Slatkine (book).

R. S. Bucks, S. Singh, J. M. Cuerden, and G. K. Wilcock. 2000. Analysis of spontaneous, conversational speech in dementia of Alzheimer type: Evaluation of an objective technique for analysing lexical performance. *Aphasiology*, 14(1):71–91, jan.

Lina Grasso, M. Carmen Díaz-Mardomingo, and Herminia Peraita-Adrados. 2011. Deterioro de la memoria semántico-conceptual en pacientes con enfermedad de Alzheimer. Análisis cualitativo y cuantitativo de los rasgos semánticos. *Psicogeriatría*, 3(4):159–165.

José María Guerrero, Rafael Martínez-Tomás, Mariano Rincón, and Herminia Peraita-Adrados. 2016. Bayesian Network Model to Sup-port Diagnosis of Cognitive Impair-ment Compatible with an Early Diagnosis of Alzheimers Disease. *Methods of Information in Medicine*, 55:42–49.

Curry Guinn and Anthony Habash. 2012. Language Analysis of Speakers with Dementia of the Alzheimer's Type. In *Association for the Advancement of Artificial Intelligence Fall Symposia*, pages 8–13. AAAI.

Curry Guinn, Ben Singer, and Anthony Habash. 2014. A comparison of syntax, semantics, and pragmatics in spoken language among residents with Alzheimer's disease in managed-care facilities. In *2014 IEEE Symposium on Computational Intelligence in Healthcare and e-health (CICARE)*, pages 98–103. IEEE, dec.

A Honoré. 1979. Some simple measures of richness of vocabulary. *Association for literary and linguistic computing bulletin*, 7(2):172–177.

William L Jarrold, Bart Peintner, Eric Yeh, Ruth Krasnow, Harold S Javitz, and Gary E Swan. 2010. Language Analytics for Assessing Brain Health : Cognitive Impairment , Depression and Pre-symptomatic Alzheimer's Disease. In Yiyu Yao, Ron Sun, Tomaso Poggio, Jiming Liu, Ning Zhong, and Jimmy Huang, editors, *Lecture Notes in Computer Science (including subseries Lecture Notes in Artificial Intelligence and Lecture Notes in Bioinformatics)*, chapter Brain Info, pages 299–307. Springer Berlin Heidelberg, Berlin, Heidelberg.

William Jarrold, Bart Peintner, David Wilkins, Dimitra Vergryi, Colleen Richey, Maria Luisa Gorno-Tempini, and Jennifer Ogar. 2014. Aided diagnosis of dementia type through computer-based analysis of spontaneous speech. In *Proceedings of the ACL Workshop on Computational Linguistics and Clinical Psychology*, pages 27–36.

Susan Kemper, Emily LaBarge, Richard Ferraro, Hintat Cheung, Him Cheung, and Martha Storandt. 1993. On the preservation of syntax in Alzheimer's disease: Evidence from written sentences. *Archives of neurology*, 50(1):81–86.

Ali Khodabakhsh, Fatih Yesil, Ekrem Guner, and Cenk Demiroglu. 2015. Evaluation of linguistic and prosodic features for detection of Alzheimer's disease in Turkish conversational speech. *EURASIP Journal on Audio, Speech, and Music Processing*, 2015(1):9, mar.

Lluís Padró and Evgeny Stanilovsky. 2012. Freeling 3.0: Towards wider multilinguality. In European Language Resources Association, editor, *Proceedings of the Language Resources and Evaluation Conference*, pages 2473–2479, Istanbul, Turkey.

Fabian Pedregosa, Gaël Varoquaux, Alexandre Gramfort, Vincent Michel, Bertrand Thirion, Olivier Grisel, Mathieu Blondel, P. Prettenhofer, R. Weiss, V. Dubourg, and J. Vanderplas. 2011. Scikit-learn: Machine learning in Python. *The Journal of Machine Learning Research*, 12:2825–2830.

Herminia Peraita and Lina Grasso. 2010. Corpus lingüístico de definiciones de categorías semánticas de personas mayores sanas y con la enfermedad del alzheimer. Technical report, Fundación BBVA.

Emily Tucker Prud'hommeaux and Brian Roark. 2011. Extraction of Narrative Recall Patterns for Neuropsychological Assessment. In *INTERSPEECH 2011, 12th Annual Conference of the International Speech Communication Association*, pages 3021–3024.

Johannes Schröder, Britta Wendelstein, and Ekkehard Felder. 2010. Language in the Preclinical Stage of Alzheimer's Disease. Content and Complexity in Biographic Interviews of the ILSE Study. In *Klinische Neurophysiologie*, volume 41, page S360.

Glenn E Smith and Mark W Bondi. 2013. *Mild Cognitive Impairment and Dementia: Definitions, Diagnosis, and Treatment*. OUP USA, illustrate edition.

Vanessa Taler and Natalie A. Phillips. 2008. Language performance in Alzheimer's disease and mild cognitive impairment: a comparative review. *Journal of clinical and experimental neuropsychology*, 30(5):501–56, jul.

Conversing with the elderly in Latin America: a new cohort for multimodal, multilingual longitudinal studies on aging

Laura Hernández-Domínguez
ÉTS, Quebec University
1100 Notre-Dame
Montreal, QC H3C1K3
laudobla
@gmail.com

Sylvie Ratté
ÉTS, Quebec Univ.
1100 Notre-Dame
Montreal, H3C1K3
Sylvie.Ratte
@etsmtl.ca

Charlene Pope
MUSC
Charleston, SC
29425-1600
popec
@musc.edu

Boyd Davis
UNC Charlotte
Charlotte,
NC 28223
bdavis
@uncc.edu

Abstract

Many studies have found that language alterations can aid in the detection of certain medical afflictions. In this work, we present an ongoing project for recollecting multilingual conversations with the elderly in Latin America. This project, so far, involves the combined efforts of psychogeriatricians, linguists, computer scientists, research nurses and geriatric caregivers from six institutions across USA, Canada, Mexico and Ecuador. The recollections are being made available to the international research community. They consist of conversations with adults aged sixty and over, with different nationalities and socio-economic backgrounds. Conversations are recorded on video, transcribed and time-aligned. Additionally, we are in the process of receiving written texts—recent or old—authored by the participants, provided voluntarily. Each participant is recorded at least twice a year to allow longitudinal studies. Furthermore, information such as medical history, educational background, economic level, occupation, medications and treatments is being registered to aid conducting research on treatment progress and pharmacological effects. Potential studies derived from this work include speech, voice, writing, discourse, and facial and corporal expression analysis. We believe that our recollections incorporate complementary data that can aid researchers in further understanding the progression of cognitive degenerative diseases of the elderly.

1 Introduction

The *Carolinas Conversations Collection* (Pope and Davis, 2011), a project for recollecting conversations with elderly people that live in North and South Carolina, started in 2008. This project was initially supported by the USA National Library of Medicine. For the collection, the conversations were transcribed, marked, time-aligned and made available to the international research community by means of a secured website[1]. The collection has grown steadily since then, having, at present, over 460 conversations with adults over sixty years old, either healthy or suffering from any medical condition. A fourth of these conversations were made with participants afflicted with Alzheimer's disease.

In 2015, we started to increase the coverage of this collection to incorporate different languages. The first additional language to be incorporated is Latin-American Spanish. We are currently adding conversations with new participants; elderly Spanish speakers from Ecuador and Mexico. Additionally, we are incorporating new information and language modalities to increase the robustness of possible studies that may use this corpus. So far, this project has engaged involvement through combined efforts of six institutions across four different countries.

2 Methodology

The recollections are being made at least twice a year with each participant. In Ecuador, we are working in collaboration with *"Universidad Técnica Particular de Loja"* (UTPL), and with the *"Perpetuo Socorro"* Foundation, a home for elderly people. In Mexico, the psychogeriatricians from the Psychiatric Hospital *"Fray Bernardino*

---

[1] http://carolinaconversations.musc.edu/

Proceedings of the 7th Workshop on Cognitive Aspects of Computational Language Learning, pages 16–21,
Berlin, Germany, August 11, 2016. ©2016 Association for Computational Linguistics

Álvarez" have agreed to work as our medical experts and advisors for this project. Furthermore, the Foundation and the Psychiatric Hospital have made arrangements to allow us to communicate with their residents, patients and their guardians, and invite them to participate in our Latin American recollections.

In the case of Ecuador, none of the involved institutions has an Institutional Review Board (IRB) for protection of human subjects, or any formal ethics guidelines. For this reason, our institutional IRB took over that role. Consequently, a person authorized via the protocol and having a Canadian or American certification of training in ethics for research with human subjects, must be present, in person, during all recollections. In the case of Mexico, the hospital has its own IRB, and their staff are trained in ethics. This allows them to recollect the conversations without any member of the team from Canada or the USA needing to be present.

Before the recordings, the participants and their caregivers are given a short explanation of the project and its aims. Provided they agree to participate in the project, they sign an informed consent form, and with the help of their primary psychiatric care providers or their primary caregiver, we fill a questionnaire with the medical information of the participant. In this questionnaire we request all the medications that the participants are actively taking, as well as their medical conditions. With first-time participants, we also record their demographic data, such as birth date, gender, educational level, occupation (prior to retirement), first language, and ethnic affiliation. To protect the privacy of the participants, all names are replaced by aliases. In the case of Ecuador, aliases are randomly chosen from a pool of names of characters or writers of classic Latin American novels; in the case of Mexico, they are chosen from names of congresspeople. We select aliases that correspond with the gender of the participants.

The interviewers are the caregivers at the Foundation (Ecuador), and the primary psychiatric care providers (Mexico). All interviews take place in the Foundation's and the psychiatric hospital's facilities. We believe that having free topics, and a familiar interviewer and environment, helps provide a more comfortable atmosphere for the participants.

All our interviewers have been trained with techniques to motivate the participants to talk, even if they are afflicted by some type of cognitive impairment. We've created animated videos and other training materials to instruct interviewers on how to incite free conversations with patients. The strategies that we provide, come from practices that have been developed during the years of experience interviewing elderly participants in North and South Carolina for this collection. These materials are available online [2] to facilitate the long-distance knowledge exchange.

While training the interviewers, we usually start by explaining the context of the project. We then emphasize the importance of letting the participants talk and express themselves as much as possible. We ask the interviewers to be patient and allow the participants some time to process their questions and then answer. We also give them cues such as repeating the last utterance of the participants when they are stuck; giving encouraging feedback and signs of interest, such as making eye contact, responding with interjections, corporal and facial expressions according to the mood of the conversation; and keeping the flow of the conversation by mentioning any information that they have gathered about the participants during the time of knowing them.

The conversations are free in the sense that there is no specific theme to talk about, although the most common topics are the early lives of the participants, their hobbies, their health and their views on life in general. There is no time limit to these conversations. Some of the common questions to start the flow of the conversation are: *"Tell us about your life"*, *"What do you like to do?"*, *"How was your childhood?"*, *"Do you have any hobbies?"*, *"Who is accompanying you today?"*, *"Do you have any pet?"*, *"What did you use to do for a living?"*.

The conversations from Mexico and Ecuador are being manually transcribed and time-aligned by our collaborators of the Linguistic Engineering Group (LEG) at the National University of Mexico. We selected the LEG group due to their vast experience in the creation of corpora[3] in Spanish. The transcriptions are labelled with markings that indicate pauses, interruptions, external noises, participant's noises (e.g., laughter, crying, coughing, hawkings), intonation and emphasis (e.g., whis-

---

[2]https://goo.gl/E7xeOO (English and Spanish subtitles are available)

[3]http://www.corpus.unam.mx/

pering, yelling), actions (e.g., winking, hand gesturing, finger snapping, clapping), and unconventional pronunciations.

In addition to the recordings of the conversations, at Mexico we are also asking the participants and/or their guardians for copies (digital or physical) of written texts, such as old letters, messages, etc., authored by the participants, recently or in years prior to this study, including letters from their youth or middle age. This is to encourage research in written analysis, such as the famous Nun Study (Snowdon et al., 1996).

3 Description of the samples

Recollections in Ecuador started in May, 2015. For the first series we interviewed 12 participants, and recorded a total of 15 conversations. The second recollection was made on January, 2016, and it incorporated 4 new participants and a total of 10 interviews. So far, the cumulative recorded time of conversations in Ecuador is over six hours and 45 minutes, and the average length of the conversations is 16 minutes. The participants' ages range from 70 to 91 years old, with an average age of 83 years old (see Table 1).

We started the recollections in Mexico in February, 2016. For these recollections, the psychiatric care providers interview the participants after their routine consultations. Therefore, all recollections and follow-ups are carried out throughout the year. While writing this paper, the recollections in Mexico have just begun and, so far, they included 9 participants, all female. However, we estimate recording at least one conversation per week. Here the participants' ages range from 61 to 82 years old, with an average age of 69 years old.

		Women	Men	Global
USA	Participants	71	16	87
	Conversations	368	94	462
	Avg. age	79.3	79.1	79.3
	Avg. education (years)	13.1	14.1	13.3
Ecuador	Participants	12	4	16
	Conversations	18	7	25
	Avg. age	83.9	83	83.6
	Avg. education (years)	6.2	8.2	6.7
Mexico	Participants	9	0	9
	Conversations	9	0	9
	Avg. age	69	-	69
	Avg. education (years)	5.5	-	5.5

Table 1: Socio-demographic overview of the participants of the collection

As shown in Table 1, the majority of our participants in all countries are female. We attribute this phenomenon to two main factors: first and foremost, women have shown a significantly higher willingness, in comparison to men, to participate in this project, especially in Mexico. Secondly, the age expectancy of women is higher than men, for which the elderly male population is smaller. We are currently making efforts to increase the number of male participants to balance the sample.

4 Implications, applications and prospects

The longitudinal, multilingual and multimodal attributes of our collection, as well as the registration and follow up of the medical treatments taken by the participants and their demographic information, will allow researchers to perform a wide variety of studies. Some of these studies have already been tackled before. However in most cases authors have used small monolingual and homogeneous samples that do not allow the possibility of generalizing. Furthermore, many of the datasets used for these studies are not shared to the research community, limiting the advancement of research.

Our collection has the advantage of containing a multiethnic sample, not to mention the heterogeneity gained by including participants from three different countries. These attributes will make for robust research that will support the study of intra-language and inter-language variations, as well as intermodal linguistic analyses (see Figure 1). Additionally, it will allow control for alterations attributable to race, demographic factors, specific diseases, medications and treatments. Longitudinal studies will allow following the course of aging in the elderly, and the differences between a healthy versus a pathological decline. This collection also provides data to improve automatic transcription and face recognition for this particular cohort, which tends to present particular challenges. Some of the clearest research possibilities to be performed with this collection are those focused on the improvement of communication with the elderly, and medical applications.

4.1 Improving communication

It is important to maintain and preserve communication with the elderly, especially since it has been suggested (Arkin, 2007) that maintaining language-enriched conversations along with exercise can delay the effects of dementia. Our col-

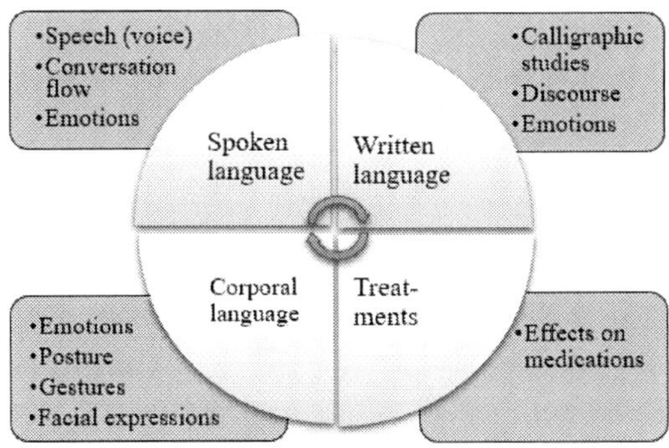

Figure 1: Multimodal studies available in the corpus.

lection not only contains the utterances and transcriptions of the elderly participants, but it also includes the entire transcription of the exchanges with the interviewers. This allows performing studies to improve communication by analyzing which strategies prove more successful in promoting conversations with the elderly. Other authors (Davis, 2005; Davis et al., 2011) have made a strong emphasis on the importance of preserving communication with elderly people, and have worked in the development of specific communication strategies, particularly with those suffering from dementia.

In addition to explicit linguistic barriers, there are other factors that limit our ability to communicate with elderly people. For example, Freudenberg et al. (2015) found out that young people have trouble correctly interpreting facial expressions in the elderly, often perceiving neutral expressions as negative emotions. This in part makes studying emotions in this population a challenge, but in doing so, could provide insights on how to preserve an effective communication with them. However, analysis of emotions have other purposes, since alterations in the expression of emotions can show signs of certain disorders (Hamm et al., 2014; Adams and Oliver, 2011).

4.2 Medical applications

Automatic language analysis for studying neurodegenerative diseases in elderly people has been gaining momentum in recent years. Authors like Jarrold et al. (2010) and (2014), Schrder et al. (2010), Prud'hommeaux and Roark, (2011), Lehr et al., (2013), Gonzalez-Moreira et al. (2014), Khodabakhsh (2014) and (2015), Guerrero et al. (2016), López-de-Ipiña

et al. (2015), and König et al. (2015), have studied language alterations that may aid in the automatic detection, or even prediction, of Mild Cognitive Impairment and Alzheimer's disease in its mild and moderate stages, with promising results. Additionally, Goberman et al. (2010), Holtgraves et al. (2013), and Cardona et al. (2013), have studied the linguistic features associated with Parkinson's disease. To support the furthering of these types of research, we prioritize the inclusion of participants suffering from different cognitive and mental afflictions (see Table 2).

	USA	Ecuador	Mexico
Participants	**87**	**16**	**9**
Alzheimer's dis.	47	8	2
Parkinson's dis.	0	1	0
Depression	9	3	1
Schizophrenia	1	0	1
Bipolar disorder	1	1	0
Healthy (cognit.)	23	5	2

Table 2: Prevalence of the main mental health disorders in each cohort.

5 Conclusions and future work

In this paper we presented a report of our first recollections of conversations with elderly people in Latin America, as well as the characteristics of this ongoing multidisciplinary multicenter research project. We envisage to continue these recollections for the following two to five years. Additionally, we are initiating the necessary collaboration agreements with Canadian institutions to incorporate a cohort with Canadian French-speakers and English-speakers to our collection. With this cohort we will add a new language and an English variation. Furthermore, in Ecuador we are making arrangements to incorporate some elderly Quechua-speakers to our sample. To our knowledge, there is no available research on linguistic analysis of this indigenous population. Finally, we are currently working on our first research using this corpus. We believe that our recollections can be of use for performing speech, voice, writing, discourse, and facial and corporal expression-based analysis to further our understanding about the progression of cognitive degenerative diseases, and ultimately to help improving our communication strategies with the elderly, thus ameliorating their quality of life.

Acknowledgments

We wish to express our deepest appreciation to all the participants of this collection and their their caregivers for their time and patience, also to the interviewers and transcribers that have greatly contributed to the creation of this dataset. We would also like to thank the Psychiatric Hospital *"Fray Bernardino Álvarez"* in Mexico City, specially Dr. Andrés Roche Bergua, Dr. Alexiz Bojorge and Dr. Janet Jiménez Genchi, for their support, clinical insights and collaboration in the creation of the Mexican cohort of the dataset. We also thank profusely all the staff members of the *"Perpetuo Socorro"* Foundation in Quito, Ecuador, specially Dr. Edwin Velasco and Mrs. Amparo Sarabia. We are also deeply grateful for the support of the Linguistic Engineering Group at the Engineering Institute at UNAM, in particular to its leader Dr. Gerardo Sierra Martínez. Finally, we would like to thank the *"Universidad Técnica Particular de Loja"* (UTPL) in Loja, Ecuador. This research was partially supported by the FRQNT 177601, and the Ministère des Relations Internationales et de la Francophonie and CONACYT Mexico (XV Groupe de Travail Québec-Mexique 2015-2017).

References

Dawn Adams and Chris Oliver. 2011. The expression and assessment of emotions and internal states in individuals with severe or profound intellectual disabilities. *Clinical psychology review*, 31(3):293–306, apr.

Sharon Arkin. 2007. Language-enriched exercise plus socialization slows cognitive decline in Alzheimer's disease. *American Journal of Alzheimer's Disease and Other Dementias*, 22(1):62–77.

Juan Felipe Cardona, Oscar Gershanik, Carlos Gelormini-Lezama, Alexander Lee Houck, Sebastian Cardona, Lucila Kargieman, Natalia Trujillo, Analía Arévalo, Lucia Amoruso, Facundo Manes, and Agustín Ibáñez. 2013. Action-verb processing in Parkinson's disease: new pathways for motor-language coupling. *Brain structure & function*, 218(6):1355–73, nov.

Boyd Davis, Margaret Maclagan, Tasos Karakostas, Simon Liang, and Dena Shenk. 2011. Watching what you say: walking and talking in dementia. *Topics in Geriatric Rehabilitation*, 27(4):268–277.

Boyd H. (ed) Davis. 2005. *Alzheimer talk, text, and context: Enhancing communication*. Palgrave Macmillan.

Maxi Freudenberg, Reginald B. Adams, Robert E. Kleck, and Ursula Hess. 2015. Through a glass darkly: facial wrinkles affect our processing of emotion in the elderly. *Frontiers in psychology*, 6.

Alexander M Goberman, Michael Blomgren, and Erika Metzger. 2010. Characteristics of speech disfluency in Parkinson disease. *Journal of Neurolinguistics*, 23(5):470–478.

E. Gonzalez-Moreira, D. Torres-Boza, M.A. Garcia-Zamora, C.A. Ferrer, and L.A. Hernandez-Gomez. 2014. Prosodic speech analysis to identify mild cognitive impairment. *VI Latin American Congress on Biomedical Engineering (CLAIB)*, pages 580–583.

José María Guerrero, Rafael Martínez-Tomás, Mariano Rincón, and Herminia Peraita-Adrados. 2016. Bayesian Network Model to Sup-port Diagnosis of Cognitive Impair-ment Compatible with an Early Diagnosis of Alzheimers Disease. *Methods of Information in Medicine*, 55:42–49.

Jihun Hamm, Amy Pinkham, Ruben C Gur, Ragini Verma, and Christian G. Kohler. 2014. Dimensional information-theoretic measurement of facial emotion expressions in schizophrenia. *Schizophrenia research and treatment*, 2014.

Thomas Holtgraves, Kelly Fogle, and Lindsay Marsh. 2013. Pragmatic language production deficits in Parkinson's disease. *Advances in Parkinson's Disease*, 2(1):31–36.

William L Jarrold, Bart Peintner, Eric Yeh, Ruth Krasnow, Harold S Javitz, and Gary E Swan. 2010. Language Analytics for Assessing Brain Health : Cognitive Impairment , Depression and Pre-symptomatic Alzheimer's Disease. In Yiyu Yao, Ron Sun, Tomaso Poggio, Jiming Liu, Ning Zhong, and Jimmy Huang, editors, *Lecture Notes in Computer Science (including subseries Lecture Notes in Artificial Intelligence and Lecture Notes in Bioinformatics)*, chapter Brain Info, pages 299–307. Springer Berlin Heidelberg, Berlin, Heidelberg.

William Jarrold, Bart Peintner, David Wilkins, Dimitra Vergryi, Colleen Richey, Maria Luisa Gorno-Tempini, and Jennifer Ogar. 2014. Aided diagnosis of dementia type through computer-based analysis of spontaneous speech. In *Proceedings of the ACL Workshop on Computational Linguistics and Clinical Psychology*, pages 27–36.

Ali Khodabakhsh, Serhan Kusxuoglu, and Cenk Demiroglu. 2014. Natural language features for detection of Alzheimer's disease in conversational speech. In *IEEE-EMBS International Conference on Biomedical and Health Informatics (BHI)*, pages 581–584. IEEE, jun.

Ali Khodabakhsh, Fatih Yesil, Ekrem Guner, and Cenk Demiroglu. 2015. Evaluation of linguistic and prosodic features for detection of Alzheimer's disease in Turkish conversational speech. *EURASIP*

Journal on Audio, Speech, and Music Processing, 2015(1):9, mar.

Alexandra König, Aharon Satt, Alexander Sorin, Ron Hoory, Orith Toledo-Ronen, Alexandre Derreumaux, Valeria Manera, Frans Verhey, Pauline Aalten, Phillipe H. Robert, and Renaud David. 2015. Automatic speech analysis for the assessment of patients with predementia and Alzheimer's disease. *Alzheimer's & Dementia: Diagnosis, Assessment & Disease Monitoring*, 1(1):112–124, mar.

Maider Lehr, Izhak Shafran, Emily Tucker Prud'hommeaux, and Brian Roark. 2013. Discriminative Joint Modeling of Lexical Variation and Acoustic Confusion for Automated Narrative Retelling Assessment. In *HLT-NAACL*, pages 211–220.

K. López-de Ipiña, J.B. Alonso-Hernández, J. Solé-Casals, C.M. Travieso-González, A. Ezeiza, M. Faúndez-Zanuy, P.M. Calvo, and B. Beitia. 2015. Feature selection for automatic analysis of emotional response based on nonlinear speech modeling suitable for diagnosis of Alzheimers disease. *Neurocomputing*, 150(PB):392–401, feb.

Charlene Pope and Boyd H. Davis. 2011. Finding a balance: The Carolinas Conversation Collection. *Corpus Linguistics and Linguistic Theory*, 7(1):143–161.

Emily Tucker Prud'hommeaux and Brian Roark. 2011. Extraction of Narrative Recall Patterns for Neuropsychological Assessment. In *INTERSPEECH 2011, 12th Annual Conference of the International Speech Communication Association*, pages 3021–3024.

Johannes Schröder, Britta Wendelstein, and Ekkehard Felder. 2010. Language in the Preclinical Stage of Alzheimer's Disease. Content and Complexity in Biographic Interviews of the ILSE Study. In *Klinische Neurophysiologie*, volume 41, page S360.

David A. Snowdon, Susan J. Kemper, James A. Mortimer, Lydia H. Greiner, David R. Wekstein, and William R. Markesbery. 1996. Linguistic ability in early life and cognitive function and Alzheimer's disease in late life: Finds from the Nun Study. *Journal of the American Medical Association*, 275(7):528–532.

Leveraging Annotators' Gaze Behaviour for Coreference Resolution

Joe Cheri Ross, Abhijit Mishra, Pushpak Bhattacharyya
Department of Computer Science & Engineering
Indian Institute of Technology Bombay, Mumbai
`{joe,abhijitmishra,pb}@cse.iitb.ac.in`

Abstract

This paper aims at utilizing cognitive information obtained from the eye movements behavior of annotators for automatic coreference resolution. We first record eye-movement behavior of multiple annotators resolving coreferences in 22 documents selected from MUC dataset. By inspecting the gaze-regression profiles of our participants, we observe how regressive saccades account for selection of potential antecedents for a certain anaphoric mention. Based on this observation, we then propose a heuristic to utilize gaze data to prune mention pairs in mention-pair model, a popular paradigm for automatic coreference resolution. Consistent improvement in accuracy across several classifiers is observed with our heuristic, demonstrating why cognitive data can be useful for a difficult task like coreference resolution.

1 Introduction

Coreference resolution deals with identifying the expressions in a discourse referring to the same entity. It is crucial to many information retrieval tasks (Elango, 2005). One of its main objectives of is to resolve the noun phrases to the entities they refer to. Though there exist many rule based (Kennedy and Boguraev, 1996; Mitkov, 1998; Raghunathan et al., 2010) and machine learning based (Soon et al., 2001; Ng and Cardie, 2002; Rahman and Ng, 2011) approaches to coreference resolution, they are way behind imitating the human process of coreference resolution. Comparing the performance of different existing systems on a standard dataset, *Ontonotes*, released for CoNLL-2012 shared task (Pradhan et al., 2012), it is quite evident that the recent systems do not have much improvement in accuracy over the earlier systems (Björkelund and Farkas, 2012; Dur-

rett and Klein, 2013; Björkelund and Kuhn, 2014; Martschat et al., 2015; Clark and Manning, 2015).

This paper attempts to gain insight into the cognitive aspects of coreference resolution to improve mention-pair model, a well-known supervised coreference resolution paradigm. For this we employ eye-tracking technology that has been quite effective in the field of psycholinguistics to study language comprehension (Rayner and Sereno, 1994), lexical (Rayner and Duffy, 1986) and syntactic processing(von der Malsburg and Vasishth, 2011). Recently, eye-tracking studies have been conducted for various language processing tasks like Sentiment Analysis, Translation and Word Sense Disambiguation. Joshi et al. (2014) develop a method to measure the sentiment annotation complexity using cognitive evidence from eye-tracking. Mishra et al. (2013) measure complexity in text to be translated based on gaze input of translators which is used to label training data. Joshi et al. (2013) propose a studied the cognitive aspects if Word Sense Disambiguation (WSD) through eye-tracking.

Eye-tracking studies have also been conducted for the task of coreference resolution. Cunnings et al. (2014) check for whether the syntax or discourse representation has better role in pronoun interpretation. Arnold et al. (2000) examine the effect of gender information and accessibility to pronoun interpretation. Vonk (1984) studies the fixation patterns on pronoun and associated verb phrases to explain comprehension of pronouns.

We perform yet another eye-tracking study to understand certain facets of human process involved in coreference resolution that eventually can help automatic coreference resolution. Our participants are given a set of documents to perform coreference annotation and the eye movements during the exercise are recorded. Eye-movement patterns are characterized by two basic attributes: (1) Fixations, corresponding to a longer stay of gaze on a visual object (like charac-

Proceedings of the 7th Workshop on Cognitive Aspects of Computational Language Learning, pages 22–26,
Berlin, Germany, August 11, 2016. ©2016 Association for Computational Linguistics

ters, words *etc.* in text) (2) Saccades, corresponding to the transition of eyes between two fixations. Moreover, a saccade is called a *Regressive Saccade* or simply, *Regression* if it represents a phenomenon of going back to a pre-visited segment. While analyzing these attributes in our dataset, we observe a correlation between the *Total Regression Count* and the complexity of a mention being resolved. Additionally, *Mention Regression Count, i.e.,* the count of a previous mention getting visited while resolving for an anaphoric mention, proves to be a measure of relevance of that particular mention as antecedent to the anaphoric mention.

Following the insights, we try to enrich mention-pair model, a popular paradigm in automatic coreference resolution by performing mention pair pruning prior to classification using mention regression data.

2   Creation of Eye-movement Database

We prepared a set of 22 short documents, each having less than 10 sentences. These were selected from the MUC-6 dataset[1]. Discourse size is restricted in order to make the task simpler for the participants and to reduce eye movements error caused due to scrolling.

The documents are annotated by 14 participants. Out of them, 12 of them are graduate/postgraduate students with science and engineering background in the age group of 20-30 years, with English as the primary language of academic instruction. The rest 2 are expert linguists and they belong to the age group of 47-50. To ensure that they possess good English proficiency, a small English comprehension test is carried out before the start of the experiment. Once they clear the comprehension test, they are given a set of instructions beforehand and are advised to seek clarifications before they proceed further. The instructions mention the nature of the task, annotation input method, and necessity of head movement minimization during the experiment.

The task given to the participants is to read one document at a time, and assign ids to mentions that are already marked in the document. Each id corresponding to a certain mention has to be unique, such that all the coreferent mentions in a single coreference chain are assigned with the

same id. During the annotation, eye movements data of the participants (in terms of fixations, saccades and pupil-size) are tracked using an SR-Research Eyelink-1000 Plus eye-tracker (monocular mode with sampling rate of 500 Hz). The eye-tracking device is calibrated at the start of each reading session. Participants are allowed to take breaks between two reading sessions, to prevent fatigue over time.

We observe that the average annotation accuracy in terms of CoNLL-score ranges between **70.75%-86.81%**. Annotation error, we believe, could be attributed to: (a) Lack of patience/attention while reading, (b) Issues related to text comprehension and understanding, and (c) Confusion/indecisiveness caused due to lack of context. The dataset is freely available for academic use[2].

3   Analysis of *Eye-regression* Profiles

The cognitive activity involved in resolving coreferences is reflected in the eye movements of the participants, especially in the movements to the previously visited words/phrases in the document, termed as *regressive saccades* or simply, *regressions*. Regression count refers to the number of times the participant has revisited a candidate antecedent mention while resolving a particular anaphoric mention. This is extracted from the eye movement events between the first gaze of the anaphoric mention under consideration and the annotation event of this mention (when participants annotate the mention with a coreferent id).

Figure 1 shows the mention position (for a given mention id) in terms of the order of the mention in the document against count of regression going out from each mention to the previous mentions. The regression count for a particular mention is averaged over all the participants. As we see, average regression count tends to increase with increase in mention id, except for some mentions which may not have required visiting to the previous mentions for resolving them. The complexity of the content in MUC-6 dataset makes the spread of the regression counts dispersed. We also observe that, towards the end of the document, participants tend to regress more to the earlier sections because of limited working memory (Calvo, 2001). This increases the number of regressions performed from mentions appearing towards the

---

[1] http://www.cs.nyu.edu/cs/faculty/ grishman/muc6.html

[2] http://www.cfilt.iitb.ac.in/cognitive-nlp/

end of the document.

It is worth noting that intra-sentential mentions that have antecedents within the same sentence (as in 'Prime Minister **Brian Mulroney** and **his** *cabinet have been briefed today*') do not generally elicit regressions. We believe, intra-sentential resolutions are connected to processing of syntactic constraints in an organized manner, as explained by the binding theory (Chomsky, 1982). Though the number of intra-sentential mentions in our dataset is low, it is evident from figure 1, that they do not account for many regressions.

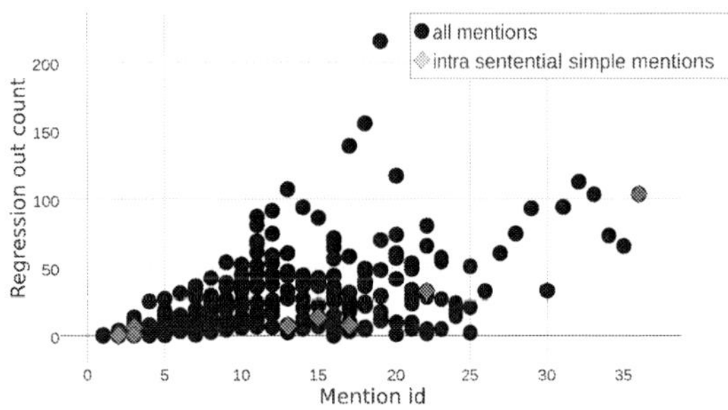

Figure 1: MUC-6 dataset: Mention id Vs Regression count

This above analysis on regression counts supports our hypothesis that the mentions that are regressed to more frequently have a better say in resolving an anaphoric mention.

4 Leveraging Cognitive Information Automatic Coreference Resolution

We experiment with a supervised system following a mention-pair model (Soon et al., 2001)- injecting the eye-movement information into it. Mention-pair model classifies mention pairs formed between mentions in a document as coreferent or not, followed by clustering, forming clusters of coreferent mentions. Eye tracking information is utilized in the process of mention pair pruning prior to mention pair classification.

4.1 For Mention-pair Pruning

Given an anaphoric mention, the probability of each previous mention being selected as antecedent is computed as follows. Transitions done by a participant to potential antecedent mentions, while resolving an anaphoric mention, are first obtained from the regression profile. From this, we filter out the regressions to a candidate antecedent

mention that happen between two events- (a) first fixation lands on the anaphoric mention and (b) the anaphoric mention gets annotated with an id.

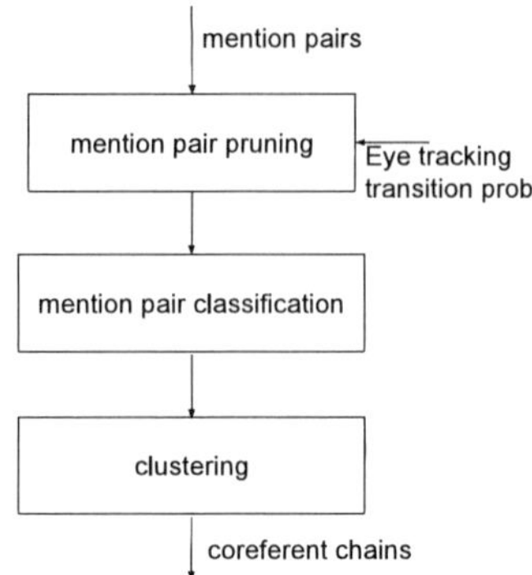

Figure 2: Mention-pair pruning

These regression counts from all the participants are aggregated to compute the transition probability values, as follows:

$$P_{m_i,m_j} = \frac{count(transitions\ m_j \rightarrow m_i)}{\sum_k count(transitions\ m_j \rightarrow m_k)}$$

(1)

In equation 1, P_{m_i,m_j} gives the transition probability value for an anaphoric mention m_j to a candidate antecedent mention m_i. count() computes the aggregated regression count over all participants. Denominator part computes for all candidate antecedents(k) of the anaphoric mention.

Transition probability thus computed for candidate mention pairs, are utilized prior to mention pair classification, filtering out irrelevant mention pairs. In the mention pair model, a mention pair(m_{ant}, m_{ana}) is formed between an anaphoric mention (m_{ana}) and a candidate antecedent mention (m_{ant}). For an anaphoric mention, the threshold probability value is computed from the number of potential candidate antecedents. $P_{thresh} = \frac{1}{\#candidate\ antecedents}$. Mentions pairs having probability less than P_{thresh} are pruned.

5 Experiments and Results

Eye movement data driven mention pair pruning, as discussed above, is experimented across different classifiers, *viz.*, Support Vector Machine (SVM), Naive Bayes, and Multi-layered Feed-Forward Neural Network (Neural Net). We use libsvm[3] for SVM implementation and Scikit-Learn[4] for Naive Bayes implementation. The neu-

---

[3]https://www.csie.ntu.edu.tw/ cjlin/libsvm/
[4]http://scikit-learn.org/

Experiments		MUC			B^3			CEAFe			CoNLL
		P	R	F	P	R	F	P	R	F	
SVM (RBF)	unpruned	61.13	68.96	64.81	57.72	75.39	65.38	47.33	58.23	52.22	**60.80**
	pruned	62.67	66.99	64.76	62.62	73.71	67.71	52.00	57.83	54.76	**62.41**
SVM (Linear)	unpruned	53.33	70.93	60.88	37.64	75.02	50.13	26.56	51.27	34.99	**48.67**
	pruned	54.71	71.42	61.96	39.63	75.07	51.88	29.44	53.14	37.89	**50.58**
Naive Bayes	unpruned	62.85	97.53	76.44	23.23	98.03	37.56	10.53	54.22	17.64	**43.88**
	pruned	62.90	96.05	76.02	25.06	96.64	39.80	13.50	58.64	21.94	**45.92**
Neural Net	unpruned	64.73	71.42	67.91	63.71	77.20	69.81	52.60	61.96	56.90	**64.87**
	pruned	66.35	70.93	68.57	66.55	76.15	71.03	55.76	62.01	58.72	**66.11**
Berkeley coref	unpruned	84.89	58.12	69.0	84.93	47.86	61.22	82.45	37.96	51.99	**60.73**
	pruned	86.86	58.62	70.0	87.15	47.64	61.6	82.7	39.26	53.25	**61.61**

Table 1: Results with different classifiers and Berkeley coreference system with and without pruning of candidate mention pairs (P,R,F)$\rightarrow$ (Precision, R:Recall, F:F-measure), CoNLL:CoNLL Score

ral network classifier having an input layer, a hidden layer and an output layer is implemented using Keras[5]. For training, we consider a subset of English section of OntoNotes (v5.0) data (Pradhan et al., 2012) with 1634 documents. Testing is done with the 22 documents taken from MUC-6 dataset.

Since the main aspect of our work is mention pair pruning, we first check the mention pair pruning accuracy. We find that mention pair pruning has a precision of **87.24%**. Pruning errors may be attributed to increased number of regressions happening to mentions towards the end of the documents (refer section 3).

Performance of the system is evaluated using MUC, B^3 and CEAFe metrics. CoNLL score is computed as the average of F1s of all the mentioned metrics. Table 1 shows the results across different classifiers with and without mention pair pruning. Considering the CoNLL score, there is an improvement in performance across all classifiers. This improvement is contributed by the increase in precision , despite the fall in recall. Table 2 shows a few instances of non-coreferent antecedent-anaphora pairs which are correctly predicted as non-coreferent because of pruning.

Antecedent	Anaphora
here	*a treaty*
Paramount Communications Inc	*an after-tax gain of $1.2 billion*
Rogers Communications	*A Spokesman*

Table 2: Instances of precision errors corrected by pruning

Among all the classifiers neural network gives better accuracy, but the effective performance gain is higher with classifiers with lesser accuracy. Naive Bayes giving the least accuracy, gives the best accuracy improvement of 2.04% with mention-pair pruning. This gives the impression that systems with lower performance, are likely to benefit from the eye movement based heuristics.

The performance improvement of mention pair pruning is also verified with the state of the art Berkeley Coreference Resolution system (Durrett and Klein, 2013). The choice of the system was based on the code accessibility to make the modification required for mention pair pruning. Results of Berkeley system in table 1 shows that there is an improvement in CoNLL score , mainly contributed by the increase in precision.

6 Conclusion and Future Work

As far as we know, our work of utilizing cognitive information for the task of automatic coreference resolution is the first of it kind. By analyzing the eye-movement patterns of annotators, we observe a correlation between the complexity of resolving an anaphoric mention and eye-regression count associated with the preceding mentions. We also observe that gaze transition probability derived from regression counts associated with a mention signify the candidacy of that mention as an antecedent. This helps us devise a heuristic to prune irrelevant mention pair candidates in a supervised coreference resolution approach. Our heuristic brings noticeable improvement in accuracy with different classifiers. The current work can be further enriched to utilize eye-gaze information for (a) meaningful feature extraction for mention pair classification and (b) proposing efficient clustering mechanism. We would also like to replace our current annotation setting with a non-intrusive reading setting (say, reading text on mobile devices with camera based eye-trackers), where explicit annotations need not be required.

---

[5] http://keras.io/

Acknowledgments

We thank for the support of CFILT lab at IIT Bombay and the annotators who helped us with coreference annotation experiment.

References

Jennifer E Arnold, Janet G Eisenband, Sarah Brown-Schmidt, and John C Trueswell. 2000. The rapid use of gender information: Evidence of the time course of pronoun resolution from eyetracking. *Cognition*, 76(1):B13–B26.

Anders Björkelund and Richárd Farkas. 2012. Data-driven multilingual coreference resolution using resolver stacking. In *Joint Conference on EMNLP and CoNLL-Shared Task*, pages 49–55. Association for Computational Linguistics.

Anders Björkelund and Jonas Kuhn. 2014. Learning structured perceptrons for coreference resolution with latent antecedents and non-local features. In *Proceedings of the Association for Computational Linguistics*.

Manuel G Calvo. 2001. Working memory and inferences: Evidence from eye fixations during reading. *Memory*, 9(4-6):365–381.

Noam Chomsky. 1982. *Some concepts and consequences of the theory of government and binding*, volume 6. MIT press.

Kevin Clark and Christopher D Manning. 2015. Entity-centric coreference resolution with model stacking. In *Association of Computational Linguistics (ACL)*.

Ian Cunnings, Clare Patterson, and Claudia Felser. 2014. Variable binding and coreference in sentence comprehension: evidence from eye movements. *Journal of Memory and Language*, 71(1):39–56.

Greg Durrett and Dan Klein. 2013. Easy victories and uphill battles in coreference resolution. In *EMNLP*, pages 1971–1982.

Pradheep Elango. 2005. Coreference resolution: A survey. *University of Wisconsin, Madison, WI*.

Salil Joshi, Diptesh Kanojia, and Pushpak Bhattacharyya. 2013. More than meets the eye: Study of human cognition in sense annotation. In *HLT-NAACL*, pages 733–738.

Aditya Joshi, Abhijit Mishra, Nivvedan Senthamilselvan, and Pushpak Bhattacharyya. 2014. Measuring sentiment annotation complexity of text. In *ACL (2)*, pages 36–41.

Christopher Kennedy and Branimir Boguraev. 1996. Anaphora for everyone: pronominal anaphora resoluation without a parser. In *Proceedings of the 16th conference on Computational linguistics-Volume 1*, pages 113–118. Association for Computational Linguistics.

Sebastian Martschat, Patrick Claus, and Michael Strube. 2015. Plug latent structures and play coreference resolution. *ACL-IJCNLP 2015*, page 61.

Abhijit Mishra, Pushpak Bhattacharyya, Michael Carl, and IBC CRITT. 2013. Automatically predicting sentence translation difficulty. In *ACL (2)*, pages 346–351.

Ruslan Mitkov. 1998. Robust pronoun resolution with limited knowledge. In *Proceedings of the 36th Annual Meeting of the Association for Computational Linguistics and 17th International Conference on Computational Linguistics-Volume 2*, pages 869–875. Association for Computational Linguistics.

Vincent Ng and Claire Cardie. 2002. Improving machine learning approaches to coreference resolution. In *Proceedings of the 40th Annual Meeting on Association for Computational Linguistics*, pages 104–111. Association for Computational Linguistics.

Sameer Pradhan, Alessandro Moschitti, Nianwen Xue, Olga Uryupina, and Yuchen Zhang. 2012. Conll-2012 shared task: Modeling multilingual unrestricted coreference in ontonotes. In *Joint Conference on EMNLP and CoNLL-Shared Task*, pages 1–40. Association for Computational Linguistics.

Karthik Raghunathan, Heeyoung Lee, Sudarshan Rangarajan, Nathanael Chambers, Mihai Surdeanu, Dan Jurafsky, and Christopher Manning. 2010. A multipass sieve for coreference resolution. In *Proceedings of the 2010 Conference on Empirical Methods in Natural Language Processing*, pages 492–501. Association for Computational Linguistics.

Altaf Rahman and Vincent Ng. 2011. Syntactic parsing for ranking-based coreference resolution. In *IJCNLP*, pages 465–473.

Keith Rayner and Susan A Duffy. 1986. Lexical complexity and fixation times in reading: Effects of word frequency, verb complexity, and lexical ambiguity. *Memory & Cognition*, 14(3):191–201.

Keith Rayner and Sara C Sereno. 1994. Eye movements in reading: Psycholinguistic studies. *Handbook of Psycholinguistics*.

Wee Meng Soon, Hwee Tou Ng, and Daniel Chung Yong Lim. 2001. A machine learning approach to coreference resolution of noun phrases. *Computational linguistics*, 27(4):521–544.

Titus von der Malsburg and Shravan Vasishth. 2011. What is the scanpath signature of syntactic reanalysis? *Journal of Memory and Language*, 65(2):109–127.

W Vonk. 1984. Eye movements during comprehension of pronouns. *Advances in Psychology*, 22:203–212.

From alignment of etymological data to phylogenetic inference via population genetics

Javad Nouri[1]   **Jukka Sirén**[3]   **Jukka Corander**[2,4]   **Roman Yangarber**[1]
[1]Department of Computer Science
[2]Department of Mathematics and Statistics
[3]Department of Biosciences
University of Helsinki, Finland
[4]Department of Biostatistics,
University of Oslo, Norway
`first.last@helsinki.fi`

Abstract

This paper presents a method for linking models for aligning linguistic etymological data with models for phylogenetic inference from population genetics. We begin with a large database of genetically related words—sets of cognates—from languages in a language family. We process the cognate sets to obtain a complete alignment of the data. We use the alignments as input to a model developed for phylogenetic reconstruction in population genetics. This is achieved via a natural novel projection of the linguistic data onto genetic primitives. As a result, we induce phylogenies based on aligned linguistic data. We place the method in the context of those reported in the literature, and illustrate its operation on data from the Uralic language family, which results in family trees that are very close to the "true" (expected) phylogenies.

1 Introduction

Recently, mathematical theory of statistical physics has been shown to unite stochastic *models* of evolution in seemingly diverse fields, such as population genetics, ecology and linguistics (Blythe and McKane, 2007; Blythe, 2009; Baxter et al., 2009; Vázquez et al., 2010). However, statistical *inference* about language evolution under such models is complicated by the practically intractable form of likelihoods for even a moderate set of languages. This calls for novel ways to probabilistic evaluation of any particular phylogenetic model and for learning the most plausible genealogies from data. In the context of population genetics, such an approach is introduced in (Sirén et al., 2011; Sirén et al.,

2013) by combining diffusion-based approximations of conditional distributions with adaptive Monte Carlo methods. In contrast to coalescent-based likelihoods, this approach enables analysis of much larger data collections, as the sufficient statistics from the data correspond under these models to the empirical allele frequencies of each population, rather than genetic characteristics of single individuals. This property makes these models attractive from the perspective of evolutionary linguistics.

The field of evolutionary linguistics, or computational etymology, addresses a range of problems, including: automatic identification of sets of cognates—genetically related words; finding genetic relations across languages in a language family; finding patterns of recurrent sound correspondence among groups of languages; reconstruction of proto-forms in ancestral (usually unobserved) languages; etc. These problems are interdependent. When approached by traditional methods, work proceeds in cycles, through iterative refinement via the *comparative method*. In our work, we take sets of cognate words as given, and focus on the problems of genetic relations and patterns of correspondence. The problem of reconstruction is also addressed, indirectly.

Based on automatically derived *pairwise* correspondences among the languages in a given corpus of cognate sets[1]—we aim to determine the overall structure of the language family. To find the correspondences, we try to find the best alignment of the complete data at the level of individual sounds—or, equivalently, symbols, since we assume that our data is phonetically transcribed.

An important aspect of our approach is that we aim to use all available data—to avoid subjective

---

[1]The creators of the input dataset posit that the elements of a cognate set derive from a common origin—a word in the ancestral proto-language.

Proceedings of the 7th Workshop on Cognitive Aspects of Computational Language Learning, pages 27–37,
Berlin, Germany, August 11, 2016. ©2016 Association for Computational Linguistics

bias, which would be inherent in selecting some subset of available data, as is sometimes done with short 50- to 200-word lists. We learn *patterns of correspondence* directly from the data, in explicit form. We let only the data determine what rules are inherent in it; i.e., we look for correspondences that are inherently encoded in a given dataset—rather than relying on externally supplied (and possibly biased) assumptions or "priors." The models assume no *a priori* knowledge or "universal" principles—e.g., no preference for aligning a symbol with itself, aligning a vowel with a vowel rather than a consonant, etc.

The main idea of the approach we are exploring here—summarized in Figure 1—is to create a bridge between the two domains: on the linguistic side, alignment of etymological data, and on the population-genetics side, phylogenetic inference. The two domains operate on different kinds of objects: in linguistics we have languages, words and sounds, whereas in genetics we have populations, individuals, and their DNA sequences, and although there are apparent similarities, it is not obvious how these can be combined. In Section 4 we formalize the problem of alignment and present some details about the alignment models we use—step B in the figure. Section 6 describes our population-genetics model for phylogenetic inference (step D). Section 5 shows how we can "glue" these two together, by means of a cross-domain projection—mapping information obtained from linguistic alignments into a form usable in population genetics (step C). In Section 7 we present some results from the combined approach, which involves building pairwise distance matrices and constructing phylogenetic trees (steps E–F). The resulting trees are compared to manually-constructed gold standards, to get an estimate of the quality of the inference pipeline.

Building phylogenetic trees by applying models from population genetics to an *alignment* of a language family has not been attempted previously, to our knowledge. In section 2 we review several approaches to etymological alignment from the last decade, and describe the data we use in our experiments, in Section 3. We conclude with a discussion and current work, in Section 8.

2 Related Work

The last 15 years have seen a surge in interest in computational modeling of language relationships, change and evolution. We have been developing a family of models for this task, called the *Etymon* models, (Wettig et al., 2011; Wettig et al., 2012; Nouri and Yangarber, 2016), etc.[2]

Methods introduced in (Kondrak, 2002), inspired by alignment in machine translation, learn one-to-one sound correspondences between words in pairs of languages. Kondrak (2003), and Wettig et al. (2011) find more complex—many-to-many—sound correspondences. These methods focus on alignment. They model the context of the sound changes in a limited way, while it is known that most evolutionary changes are conditioned on the context of the evolving sound. Bouchard-Côté et al. (2007) propose MCMC-based methods to model context, and operate on more than one pair of languages at a time.[3]

The Etymon models, similarly to other work, operate at the phonetic level only, leaving semantic judgements to the creators of the input databases. Some prior work has attempted to approach semantics by computational means as well. We do not address the problem of discovering cognates; this problem is attempted, e.g., in, (Kondrak, 2004; Kessler, 2001; Steiner et al., 2011) and semi-automatically in (Bouchard-Côté et al., 2007). Our Etymon models begin with a set of etymological data (or more than one such set) for a language family as given, and treat the given cognate set as a fundamental unit of input. We use the principle of *recurrent sound correspondence*, as in much of the literature, including (Kondrak, 2002; Kondrak, 2003), and others.

One approach to evaluating our alignment models, is to try to infer relationships among entire languages within the family. Construction of phylogenies is studied extensively, e.g., by (Nakhleh et al., 2005; Ringe et al., 2002; Barbançon et al., 2009). This work differs from ours in that it operates on manually pre-compiled sets of *characters*. Each character is a distinctive feature of languages, which takes on different values among different languages within the family. All Etymon models operate at the level of sounds within words and cognate sets.

There is extensive work on alignment in the machine-translation (MT) literature, with some

---

[2]Please see *http://etymon.cs.helsinki.fi/* for the publicly available software packages.

[3]The running time did not scale well when the number of languages was above three; (Bouchard-Côté et al., 2009) describe improved models to align multiple languages.

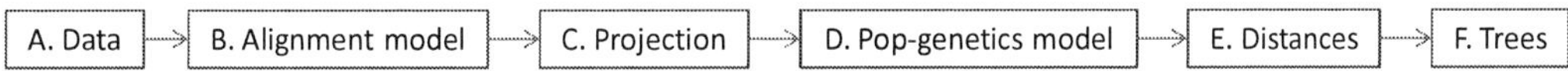

Figure 1: Outline of the components in the inference pipeline

methods from MT alignment projected onto alignment in etymology. The intuition is that sentences that are translation of each other in MT correspond to cognate words in etymology, and words in MT correspond to sounds in etymology. The notion of regularity of sound change in etymology, which is what our models try to capture, is loosely similar to contextually conditioned correspondence of translation words across languages. For example, (Kondrak, 2002) employs MT alignment from (Melamed, 1997; Melamed, 2000). One might employ the IBM models for MT alignment, (Brown et al., 1993), or the HMM model, (Vogel et al., 1996). Among the MT-related models, (Bodrumlu et al., 2009) is similar to ours in that it is based on MDL, the Minimum Description Length principle. There are important differences between our alignment problem vs. alignment in MT. Evolutionary sound correspondence is conditioned by local context, whereas in MT correspondences may depend on much wider context. There is no analogue to the notion of phonetic *features* in MT. Phonetic correspondences in etymological data—which apply throughout the language—have no analogue in semantic shift processes in a such way as to be captured by MT alignment models. Neither are phonetic features used in the aforementioned work from the area of automatic transliteration, e.g., (Zelenko, 2009).

Our work on the Etymon models is closely related to a series of generative models in (Bouchard-Côté et al., 2007) through (Hall and Klein, 2011), in the following respects.

In (Wettig et al., 2011) some context is modeled in the form of coding pairs of symbols, as in (Kondrak, 2003). Bouchard-Côté et al. (2007) and Hall and Klein (2011) handle context by conditioning the symbol being generated upon the symbols immediately preceding and following. Wettig et al. (2012) and Nouri and Yangarber (2016) use much broader context by building decision trees, so that non-relevant context information does not grow model complexity.

In (Wettig et al., 2011) sounds / symbols are treated as atomic—not analyzed in terms of their phonetic makeup. (Bouchard-Côté et al., 2007)

recognize "natural classes" in defining the context of a sound change, though not in generating the symbols themselves; (Bouchard-Côté et al., 2009) encode as a prior which sounds are "close" to each other. In (Wettig et al., 2012) and later Etymon models, we code each sound in terms of the individual phonetic features that make up the sound.

Etymon models are based on the information-theoretic MDL principle, e.g., (Grünwald, 2007)—like (Wettig et al., 2011) and unlike (Bouchard-Côté et al., 2007; Hall and Klein, 2011). MDL brings important theoretical benefits, since models chosen in this way are guided by data with no free parameters or hand-picked "priors." The data analyst chooses the model class and structure, and the coding scheme, i.e., a *decodable* way to encode both model and data. This determines the learning strategy—we optimize the cost function, which is the code length determined by these choices.

Objective function: For the objective function to optimize during alignment, we use the prequential code-length (Dawid, 1984), as explained in (Wettig et al., 2011). Normalized Maximum Likelihood (NML) as presented in (Wettig et al., 2012; Nouri and Yangarber, 2016) could be used as an alternative to prequential coding. Although NML reduces the code length, and brings other advantages, it did not have a significant effect on the quality of the alignments required in the experiments presented here.

Some of our work on modeling language change and evolution, (Nouri and Yangarber, 2016) shows that alignment may not be a necessary goal for obtaining efficient compression; in case of models that circumvent alignment, it is less clear how they can be combined with population-genetics models.

Additional prior work related to the population-genetics models is referenced throughout the paper and in Section 6.

3 Data

As we mentioned, we aim to use large-scale etymological databases, rather than small, manually-selected sets of characters of the languages. For

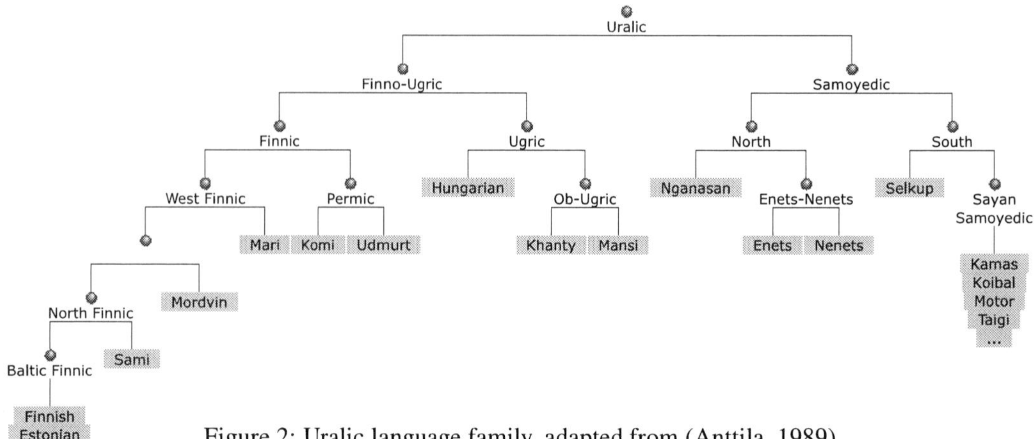

Figure 2: Uralic language family, adapted from (Anttila, 1989)

```
*Proto   k   a   r   .   n   e   š       v   e   n   e   š
         |   |   |   |   |   |   |       |   |   |   |   |
Finnish  k   ā   r   .   n   e   .       v   e   n   e   .
         |   |   |   |   |   |   |       |   |   |   |   |
Mordvin  k   .   r   e   n   .   č       v   e   n   .   č
```

Figure 3: Sample alignments for Finnish and Mordvin: *kaarne/krenč* 'raven', *vene/venč* 'boat', with unobserved, hypothesized proto word-forms

the Uralic language family, we use the Star-Ling Uralic database, (Starostin, 2005), based on (Rédei, 1991) and expanded. The database contains 2586 Uralic cognate sets. Whereas much of the prior work is based on small manually preselected subsets of the data—so-called "Swadesh lists" of 100 (or 40, 50, etc.) words—we use complete large data sets. In this paper, we focus on a sub-tree of Uralic, viz., the Finno-Ugric sub-family—i.e., excluding the remaining Samoyedic sub-tree of Uralic—which contains most of the extant Uralic data. Our experiments use the 10 "principal" Finno-Ugric languages.[4]

One arrangement of the Uralic languages accepted by some linguists is shown in Figure 2, adapted from Encyclopedia Britannica and (Anttila, 1989). Note, that this is the subject of some debate in modern scholarship, and alternative phylogenies have some acceptance among linguists. Figure 2 shows the phylogeny most widely accepted today. Other theories, e.g., posit a "Volgaic" branch, which groups together Mari with Mordvin languages, where this phylogeny posits Mari on an independent branch, an offshoot from the "West Finnic" subgroup, see, e.g., (Anttila, 1989). We use this phylogeny as a gold-standard in our experiments.

In our experiments we need a measure of distance between phylogenies proposed by different approaches. For comparison, we can treat the phylogenies as *unrooted*, leaf-labeled (URLL) trees. One distance measure for URLL trees is introduced in (Robinson and Foulds, 1981). Based on this particular distance measure, the distance between the gold standard tree and the tree with a Volgaic branch would be 0.14, (see discussion in Section 7).

4 Pairwise Alignment

We use our Etymon models, described in (Wettig et al., 2011; Wettig et al., 2012), for aligning the etymological data.e summarize the main features of these models in this section. We begin with pairwise alignment: aligning words from two languages at a time. For each word pair, the task of alignment means finding exactly which symbols correspond. The simplest form of such alignment at the symbol level is a 1-1 pair $(\sigma : \tau) \in \Sigma \times T$, a single symbol σ from the *source alphabet* Σ with a symbol τ from the *target alphabet* T. We denote the sizes of the alphabets by $|\Sigma|$ and $|T|$.

To model *insertions* and *deletions*, we augment both alphabets with a special empty symbol—denoted by a dot—and write the augmented alphabets as $\Sigma^{\cdot}$ and $T^{\cdot}$. We can then align word pairs,

---

[4]The 10 Finno-Ugric languages used in the experiments are: est=Estonian, fin=Finnish, khn=Khanty, kom=Komi, man=Mansi, mar=Mari, mrd=Mordvin, saa=Saami, udm=Udmurt, unk/ugr=Hungarian. The StarLing database also contains data on dialects for the 7 languages excluding {fin, est, unk}; in the figures, the suffix after the code identifies the *principal* dialect—having the largest number of entries in StarLing. Some of these dialects are quite far apart; in other experiments we also use the second-largest dialects, giving 17 languages in total.

such as *vene—venč* ("boat" in Finnish and Mordvin), in many ways, including, e.g., as in Figure 3, where the alignment on the right contains symbol pairs: $(v : v), (e : e), (n : n), (e : .), (. : č)$. Note that, since the Proto language is not observed, the alignment model might actually prefer to align (e:č) in these examples, especially if this pattern appears several times (which it does)—since there is no *a priori* penalty for vowel-consonant alignment, as mentioned in the Introduction.

If we align all languages simultaneously, rather than pairwise, there may be additional information in *other* languages (which there is), that may help the model disfavor (e:č). N-way alignment will be revisited in the conclusion.

According to the MDL Principle, the aim is to code these aligned word pairs as compactly as possible. To construct such a code, we "transmit" the aligned data by listing the "events"—the observed symbol pairs $(\sigma : \tau)$. Since the code needs to be uniquely decodable, after each word pair we transmit a special event $(\# : \#)$ to mark the word boundaries. The code length (or cost) for the *complete*, aligned data is our objective function that the algorithm optimizes. Lower code-length means that the algorithm has found a way of aligning the data that is more compact, i.e., it has discovered more regularity in the data.

Using prequential coding, or Bayesian Marginal Likelihood, the total cost of coding the aligned data is given by:

$$L(D) = \tag{1}$$
$$- \sum_{e \in E} \log \Gamma\big(C(e) + \alpha(e)\big) + \sum_{e \in E} \log \Gamma\big(\alpha(e)\big)$$
$$+ \log \Gamma\left[\sum_{e \in E} \big(C(e) + \alpha(e)\big) \right] - \log \Gamma\left[\sum_{e \in E} \alpha(e) \right]$$

where $E = \Sigma \cdot \times T \cdot \cup \{(\# : \#)\}$ is the event space, $C(e)$ stores the number of times event e occurs in the complete alignment, and $\alpha(e) = 1$ are the uniform Dirichlet priors.

Learning the model from the observed data now means iteratively re-aligning word pairs, and updating the matrix C, which stores the counts of all observed alignment events. The sparser C becomes, the lower the code-length will be.

Summary of the Algorithm: We start with an initial *random* alignment for each pair of words in the corpus. We then alternate between two steps: **A.** update the count matrix and compute the code length, and **B.** re-align all word pairs in the corpus, using dynamic-programming re-alignment. During the dynamic-programming step, for each word pair we find the best alignment, i.e., the one with the lowest cost given the alignments for rest of the words. The algorithm is described in detail in (Wettig et al., 2011).

The algorithm is similar to Expectation-Maximization (EM), but is in fact greedy. The iterative steps monotonically decrease the cost function, and thus compress the data. We continue until we reach convergence. To avoid local optima, we use Simulated Annealing.

5 Projection

To be able to apply phylogenetic reconstruction methods from population genetics we need to define appropriate analogues for the notions of *population*, *individual*, *locus*, and *allele*, which are the essential inputs to the population genetics models, described in the next section.

It is natural to identify population with *language*, and individuals with *words* in the language. Next, suppose that the proto-language L^* (the root of the family tree) had been fully observed, as in Figure 3. Then, for any leaf language L_i, we could align L_i to L^* (pairwise). We could then fix the set of sounds of L^* as the set of "*loci*" (sites) in the "DNA" of the individuals. We treat each sound s of L^* as a locus, in the sense that from the complete alignment from L_i to L^* we can observe the distribution of sounds (from L_i's alphabet) that were aligned to s. Thus, the *alleles* are the various sounds (in L_i's alphabet) which appear aligned to s in the words in L_i. Each L_i will have its distinctive distribution of alleles at each locus. Thus, in the Mordvin examples in Figure 3, at the "locus" labeled e in the Proto-language, we would observe the "allele" e once, and the allele *dot* twice.

However, in general, we have no access to L^*, and we proceed indirectly as follows. Suppose, for instance, $\{L_i\}$ are the 10 languages from the Finno-Ugric sub-family of Uralic. We designate each L_i, in turn, as a *reference* language—in place of the unobserved L^*. The reference L_i "donates" its sounds as the loci, to be aligned to each of the remaining 9 (*target*) languages. As before (with L^*), at each site, a target population L_j has a distinctive distribution over the *alleles*—symbols drawn from the **universal** phonetic alphabet, which is simply the union of the individual alphabets. In this way, each reference language L_i induces one dataset D^{L_i} of allele distributions in the remaining 9 populations, giving a total of 10 input datasets. These datasets are processed by the population genetics model introduced below.

Although "sacrificing" the reference language in this way skews the dataset, we compensate for this by averaging the estimated pairwise distances over *all* 10 datasets $\{D^{L_i}\}$. When we calculate the distances of languages based on a single reference, there will be a higher level of variance in the estimates and as a consequence Neighbor-Join and similar algorithms can easily lead to incorrect trees. When we instead calculate the average distance for any pair of languages (L_i, L_j) over the 8 remaining references, the variance in the estimates stabilizes (because the mean distance estimate will be much less variable) and consequently the NeighborJoin algorithm shows more accurate performance. To verify empirically these basic statistical arguments—that using the mean distances is more stable than any single estimate— we ran simulations with artificial data sets (Figure 4). In the simulation we perturb the pairwise distances with Normal noise, using mean 0 and σ as shown on the X-axis. The upper curve is the (average) URLL distance from trees built on single estimates to the gold-standard tree in Figure 2; the lower curve is the URLL distance from the tree based on the mean of the estimates to the gold-standard tree. The figures confirm the higher stability of the mean (of 8 estimates in A, 15 estimates in B), as compared to any single estimate, which is according to the expectations. In addition, there may be a small effect caused by the fact that some reference language can produce slightly better results than another, but the main effect should be the one explained above.

6   Population genetics model

With this definition of population, individual, locus, and allele, we proceed to the method for building the phylogenetic tree based on each complete aligned data set. Below we introduce expressions for conditional distributions that jointly determine a hierarchical probability model for the count data derived from the alignment. The model reflects the degree of relatedness among the languages through a tree topology and the corre-

sponding branch length parameters.[5] We consider modeling the relatedness of K languages by a rooted bifurcating tree topology T representing the order of divergence from a common ancestral language. The leaves of the topology T correspond to the K modern (observed) languages, whereas the inner nodes correspond to ancestral (unobserved) languages. The length of each branch c of T is a parameter to be inferred from the output of the alignment algorithm using the introduced two-part coding approach. Our Beta-Dirichlet model describes stochastic changes in the alignment patterns of loci by separating the shared alleles S among two or more languages from those that are present in a single language only (private alleles P). From the perspective of genetics, the latter correspond to novel mutations that arise over time in any particular population and are not observed elsewhere. For a locus, the conditional distribution of alleles for a node c of T, either observed or ancestral, is determined by the relative frequencies ψ_{Sc} and ψ_{Pc} of values in S and P, respectively. Here $\psi_{Sc} = (\psi_{Sc1}, \ldots, \psi_{Scr})$ is a vector of relative frequencies for the r alleles in S and ψ_{Pc} is a scalar of the total relative frequency of alleles in P, so that $\psi_{Pc} + \sum_{j=1}^{r} \psi_{Scj} = 1$. By definition, ψ_{Pc_a} equals zero for the root node c_a.

For each node c except the root, the conditional distribution of the relative frequency of the values in the private set ψ_{Pc} given the relative frequency $\psi_{Ppa(c)}$ in the parent node $pa(c)$ is defined as the Beta distribution:

$$\psi_{Pc} \mid \psi_{Ppa(c)} \sim Beta(\phi_{Pc}\mu_{Pc}, \phi_{Pc}(1 - \mu_{Pc})) \tag{2}$$

where μ_{Pc} corresponds to the mean of the distribution and ϕ_{Pc} determines the variance, given by

$$Var(\psi_{Pc}) = \frac{\mu_{Pc}(1 - \mu_{Pc})}{\phi_{Pc} + 1}$$

The relative frequencies of the shared features ψ_{Sc} have the conditional distribution:

$$(1 - \psi_{Pc})^{-1}\psi_{Sc} \mid \psi_{Pc}, \psi_{Ppa(c)}, \psi_{Spa(c)} \sim$$
$$\sim Dirichlet(\phi_{Sc}\mu_{Sc1}, \ldots, \phi_{Sc}\mu_{Scr}) \tag{3}$$

where again μ_{Scj} and ϕ_{Sc} control the first two central moments of the distribution.

---

[5]The underlying theory relies on concepts from theoretical population genetics, (Ewens, 2004; Blythe and McKane, 2007); the reader may refer also to (Sirén et al., 2011; Sirén et al., 2013), for a detailed account of the model structure.

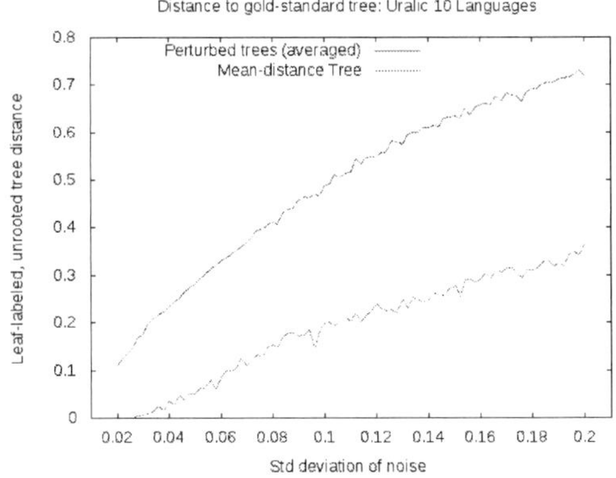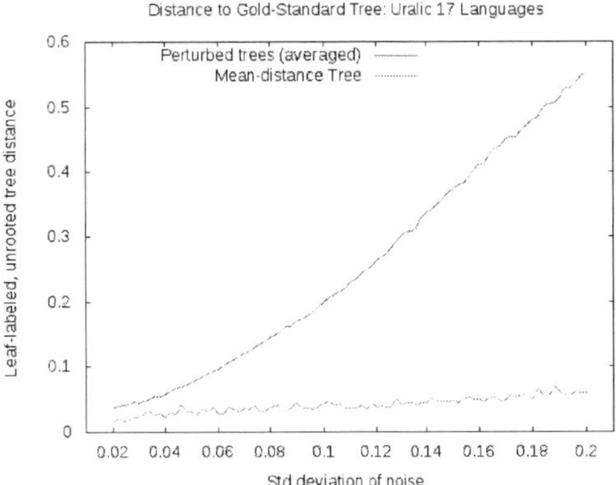

Figure 4: Stability of phylogeny based on sample means of pairwise distances vs. individual samples: (A) for 10 Uralic languages; (B) for 17 Uralic languages

We choose parameters of the two distributions as

$$\mu_{Pc} = 1 - e^{-m_c \tau_c}\bigl(1 - \psi_{Ppa(c)}\bigr) \tag{4}$$

$$\mu_{Scj} = \frac{\psi_{Spa(c)j}}{1 - \psi_{Ppa(c)}} \tag{5}$$

$$\phi_{Pc} = \frac{\mu_{Pc}}{\frac{(1-e^{-(m_c+1)\tau_c})}{(m_c+1)} - (1-\mu_{Pc})(1-e^{-\tau_c})} - 1 \tag{6}$$

$$\phi_{Sc} = \frac{(m_c + 1)(1 - \mu_{Pc})e^{-\tau_c}}{1 - e^{-(m_c+1)\tau_c}} \tag{7}$$

to yield the same expectation and covariance structure as obtained under the Wright-Fisher infinite alleles model (Sirén et al., 2013; Ewens, 2004). The parameter τ_c represents the relative time between a node and its ancestral language and m_c is an effective mutation parameter in the branch connecting c and $pa(c)$. For the relative frequencies ψ_{Sc_a} in the root node c_a, a uniform distribution is assumed in the model. Assuming conditional independence of all loci for which count data is derived in the alignment, a product multinomial distribution is obtained for the feature counts conditionally on the unknown relative frequency parameters, such that

$$p(\mathbf{x}|\psi) = \prod_{l=1}^{L} \prod_{c=1}^{K} p(\mathbf{x}_l^{(c)}|\psi_{lPc}, \psi_{lSc}), \tag{8}$$

where $p(\mathbf{x}_l^{(c)}|\psi_{lPc}, \psi_{lSc})$ is the joint multinomial probability of the feature counts $\mathbf{x}_l^{(c)}$ for the locus l in language c, where the relative frequencies are now indexed. Notice that the remaining parameters in 2 and 3 are set to be constant over the loci, thus representing the average tendency over the loci.

In our fully Bayesian probabilistic formulation, prior distributions are assigned to all the unknown parameters. Similar to (Sirén et al., 2013), here we have used uniform distributions on the interval $(0, 1)$ for the time parameters τ and exponential distributions with mean 1 for the relative mutation parameters m. As in Bayesian phylogenetics in general, the tree topologies are assigned a uniform prior distribution. These choices have been made to specify vaguely informative prior distributions which should not have any considerable effect on the resulting posterior inferences.

Using the implementation from (Sirén et al., 2013), the Adaptive Metropolis (AM) algorithm, (Haario et al., 2001) can be applied to generate samples from the conditional posterior distribution of τ, m and ψ, given a topology T and the partition of the features to sets P and S. In our MCMC simulations we used 100000 iterations in total, out of which the initial sequence of 20000 iterations was discarded as burn-in and the chain was thinned by including every 8th iteration in the final sample. This resulted in posterior samples of size 10000 values.

Here, the AM algorithm is first used to generate the posterior samples separately for each pair of languages in a given alignment, which allows us to compute the distance between the two languages as the sum of relative times τ since the divergence from a common ancestral language. Then, we construct the tree topology corresponding to the particular alignment by finding the unrooted binary tree using the neighbour joining al-

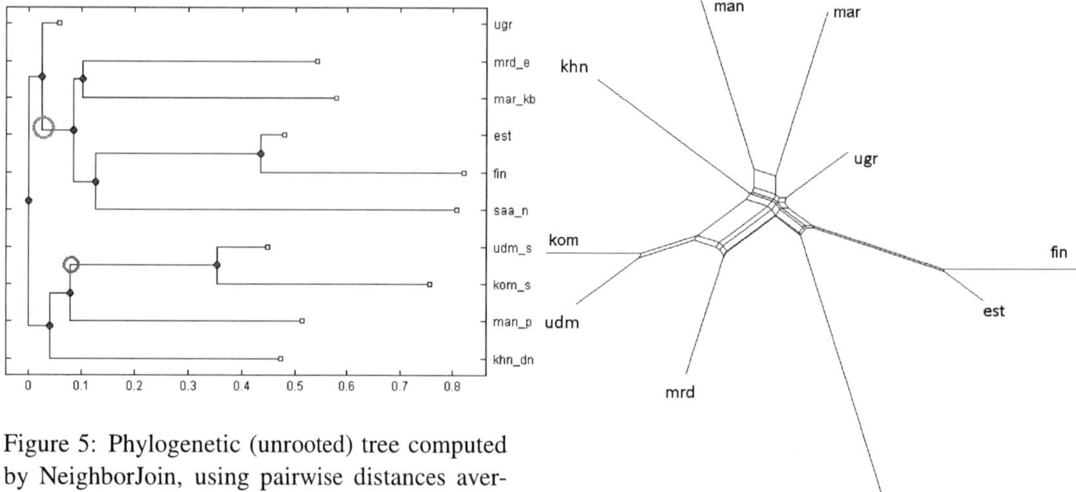

Figure 5: Phylogenetic (unrooted) tree computed by NeighborJoin, using pairwise distances averaged over 10 Uralic datasets.

Figure 6: Phylogenetic network computed by NeighborNet, using same datasets.

	D(T,G)	Count	% of Total
	0.000000	1	0.0000
	0.142857	14	0.0007
	0.285714	126	0.0062
	0.428571	1018	0.0502
	0.571429	8114	0.4003
	0.714286	60444	2.9819
	0.857143	363112	17.9135
	1.000000	1594196	78.6471
Total		2027025	

Table 1: URLL tree distances from gold standard.

gorithm, (Felsenstein, 2004). Finally, a summary tree for all languages is obtained by combining the information over all considered alignments. As the described procedure is used separately for each sample obtained from the posterior distribution of the pairwise distances, it results in a measure of statistical uncertainty associated with the topology by counting the relative number of times the obtained tree has a certain topology. Conditional on any topology constructed in this manner, one can obtain posterior inferences for its branch lengths directly from the posterior samples by including the fraction of samples leading to the particular topology.

The software suite implementing this model has been made available to the public.[6]

7   Experiments

In this section we present some results from using the combined pipeline approach, summarized in Figure 1, applied to the Uralic data.

Since we have 10 input datasets that each contribute different pairwise distances, we average these distances over all 10 datasets (for each language pair (a, b), averaging over the 8 datasets where neither a nor b is reference). A topology obtained using this method is shown in Figure 5. Recall, that this tree is *unrooted*,[7] and identifying the node circled in green with the *Finno-*

Ugric node in "gold-standard" Uralic trees yields a strong resemblance to the "true" topology. The main deviation in the derived topology is at the node circled in red, corresponding to Permic (ancestor of Komi and Udmurt), which "should" be in the other subtree relative to the Finno-Ugric root. This resulting tree has a URLL distance of 0.28 from the gold-standard tree we introduced in Section 3. To get an intuitive sense of the quality of this result, we observe that the number of unrooted leaf-labeled trees with n nodes is $(2n - 3)!!$, (see, e.g., (Ford, 2010)), which is over 2 million for 10 nodes. These trees and their distance from the gold-standard are summarized in Table 1. In the table, $D(T, G)$ denotes the distance of a selected tree to the gold standard. It is easy to check that the expected distance for a randomly selected URLL 10-leaf tree from is over 0.963, with a standard deviation of 0.17. The chance of picking a tree with distance 0.28 or less at random is under 7×10^{-5}.

---

[6]URL: *http://www.helsinki.fi/bsg/*. Compatibility between the etymological and the population-genetic suites will be maintained also in future releases.

[7]NeighborJoin selects the root via a heuristic, which only tries to minimize the length of the longest root-to-leaf path.

For a deeper investigation of the relations among the languages, we generate a phylogenetic network in SplitsTree4, (Huson and Bryant, 2006), (Figure 6), from the posterior expectations of the pair-wise distances using the Neighbor-Net method, (Bryant and Moulton, 2004). As described in the original article, (Bryant and Moulton, 2004), the sizes of the boxes in the center of the network represent uncertainty about the phylogenetic position of the adjacent leaf nodes. For instance, there is negligible uncertainty about the position of the common ancestor of Finnish and Estonian. In contrast, the greatest uncertainty is related to the position of Permic, which is the only branch in the tree in Figure 5 that deviates from the gold-standard structure. The relevance of the introduced alignment method is highlighted by the fact that our reconstruction of the language relatedness in terms of trees yields results highly congruent with gold-standards .

8 Discussion and current work

Using recent advances from population genetics, we have obtained a promising approach to fully probabilistic inference about language genealogies based on unsupervised etymological alignment. According to our knowledge, this work represent a first attempt to do such inference and it will be of considerable interest to investigate further the properties of this model family in the linguistics context. The essential elements that enable the use of a powerful population-genetics modeling approach are: a. the mapping of sounds to genetic loci which allow the use of a distribution to represent the evidence in the data; b. use of each language in turn as a *reference* language in the pair-wise alignment, instead of an (unobserved) proto-language. Since the model-based distances are averaged over a set of reference languages, the resulting distance estimates are considerably more stable than the individual estimates, as demonstrated in our numerical experiments; c. the novel diffusion approximation-based population-genetics models offer an enormous computational advantage over standard coalescent likelihood-based models. Moreover, the latter models would be considerably more difficult to adapt to the linguistic setting, since they are by definition individual-based, in contrast to the models used here, which enable a direct modeling of languages as a whole by frequencies of the mapped sounds.

Current work includes using context of sounds in aligning the word pairs, and applications to etymological data sets from other language families, and extension for modeling of *internal* nodes in the tree. One direction is using Turkic data (from StarLing), where some of the ancestral languages *are* observed, and examining how accurately the model identifies these languages with internal nodes of the phylogeny. We are also extending the presented model to work with more than 1-1 symbol alignment, using, e.g., 2-2 alignments found in (Kondrak, 2003; Wettig et al., 2012). Finally, using methods for direct N-way alignment—e.g., as suggested in (Steiner et al., 2011)—we may be able to obtain useful estimates of the sounds in the hidden Proto-language, and how they align to sounds in the observed languages. This would in a sense provide the "true" sites, and allow us to circumvent the need for averaging over distances obtained from alignment to reference languages, potentially improving the overall accuracy.

Acknowledgments

This research was supported in part by the Fin-UgRevita and Uralink Projects of the Academy of Finland, and by the National Centre of Excellence "ALGODAN: Algorithmic Data Analysis" of the Academy of Finland. We thank Teemu Roos for his assistance, and Hannes Wettig, who contributed to building the original alignment models.

References

Raimo Anttila. 1989. *Historical and comparative linguistics*. John Benjamins.

François G. Barbançon, Tandy Warnow, Don Ringe, Steven N. Evans, and Luay Nakhleh. 2009. An experimental study comparing linguistic phylogenetic reconstruction methods. In *Proceedings of the Conference on Languages and Genes*, UC Santa Barbara. Cambridge University Press.

Gareth J. Baxter, Richard A. Blythe, William Croft, and Alan J. McKane. 2009. Modeling language change: An evaluation of Trudgill's theory of the emergence of New Zealand English. *Language Variation and Change*, 21(2):257–296.

Richard A. Blythe and Alan J. McKane. 2007. Stochastic models of evolution in genetics, ecology and linguistics. *Journal of Statistical Mechanics: Theory and Experiment*, 2007:P07018.

Richard A. Blythe. 2009. Generic modes of consensus formation in stochastic language dynamics. *Journal of Statistical Mechanics: Theory and Experiment*, 2009:P02059.

Tugba Bodrumlu, Kevin Knight, and Sujith Ravi. 2009. A new objective function for word alignment. In *Proc. NAACL Workshop on Integer Linear Programming for NLP*, pages 169–174, Copenhagen, Denmark.

Alexandre Bouchard-Côté, Percy Liang, Thomas Griffiths, and Dan Klein. 2007. A probabilistic approach to diachronic phonology. In *Proceedings of the Joint Conference on Empirical Methods in Natural Language Processing and Computational Natural Language Learning (EMNLP-CoNLL:2007)*, pages 887–896, Prague, Czech Republic.

Alexandre Bouchard-Côté, Thomas L. Griffiths, and Dan Klein. 2009. Improved reconstruction of protolanguage word forms. In *Proceedings of the North American Chapter of the Association for Computational Linguistics (NAACL09)*.

Peter F. Brown, Vincent J. Della Pietra, Stephen A. Della Pietra, and Robert. L. Mercer. 1993. The mathematics of statistical machine translation: Parameter estimation. *Computational Linguistics*, 19(2):263–311.

David Bryant and Vincent Moulton. 2004. Neighbor-net: an agglomerative method for the construction of phylogenetic networks. *Molecular biology and evolution*, 21(2):255–265.

A.P. Dawid. 1984. Statistical theory: The prequential approach. *Journal of the Royal Statistical Society, Series A*, 147(2):278–292.

Warren J. Ewens. 2004. *Mathematical population genetics: theoretical introduction*, volume 1. Springer Verlag.

Joseph Felsenstein. 2004. *Inferring phylogenies*. Sunderland, Massachusetts: Sinauer Associates.

Daniel J. Ford. 2010. Encodings of cladograms and labeled trees. *Electronic Journal of Combinatorics*, 17:1556–1558.

Peter Grünwald. 2007. *The Minimum Description Length Principle*. MIT Press.

Heikki Haario, Eero Saksman, and Johanna Tamminen. 2001. An adaptive Metropolis algorithm. *Bernoulli*, 7(2):223–242.

David Hall and Dan Klein. 2011. Large-scale cognate recovery. In *Empirical Methods in Natural Language Processing (EMNLP)*.

Daniel H. Huson and David Bryant. 2006. Application of phylogenetic networks in evolutionary studies. *Molecular biology and evolution*, 23(2):254–267.

Brett Kessler. 2001. *The Significance of Word Lists: Statistical Tests for Investigating Historical Connections Between Languages*. The University of Chicago Press, Stanford, CA.

Grzegorz Kondrak. 2002. Determining recurrent sound correspondences by inducing translation models. In *Proceedings of COLING 2002: 19th International Conference on Computational Linguistics*, pages 488–494, Taipei.

Grzegorz Kondrak. 2003. Identifying complex sound correspondences in bilingual wordlists. In A. Gelbukh, editor, *Computational Linguistics and Intelligent Text Processing (CICLing-2003)*, pages 432–443, Mexico City. Springer-Verlag Lecture Notes in Computer Science, No. 2588.

Grzegorz Kondrak. 2004. Combining evidence in cognate identification. In *Proceedings of the Seventeenth Canadian Conference on Artificial Intelligence (Canadian AI 2004)*, pages 44–59, London, Ontario. Lecture Notes in Computer Science 3060, Springer-Verlag.

I. Dan Melamed. 1997. Automatic discovery of noncompositional compounds in parallel data. In *The Second Conference on Empirical Methods in Natural Language Processing*, pages 97–108, Hissar, Bulgaria.

I. Dan Melamed. 2000. Models of translational equivalence among words. *Computational Linguistics*, 26(2):221–249.

Luay Nakhleh, Don Ringe, and Tandy Warnow. 2005. Perfect phylogenetic networks: A new methodology for reconstructing the evolutionary history of natural languages. *Language (Journal of the Linguistic Society of America)*, 81(2):382–420.

Javad Nouri and Roman Yangarber. 2016. Modeling language evolution with codes that utilize context and phonetic features. In *Proceedings of CoNLL: Conference on Computational Natural Language Learning, at ACL-2016*, Berlin, Germany, August. Association for Computational Linguistics.

Károly Rédei. 1991. *Uralisches etymologisches Wörterbuch*. Harrassowitz, Wiesbaden.

Don Ringe, Tandy Warnow, and A. Taylor. 2002. Indo-European and computational cladistics. *Transactions of the Philological Society*, 100(1):59–129.

D.F. Robinson and L.R. Foulds. 1981. Comparison of phylogenetic trees. *Mathematical Biosciences*, 53(1–2):131–147.

Jukka Sirén, Pekka Marttinen, and Jukka Corander. 2011. Reconstructing population histories from single nucleotide polymorphism data. *Molecular Biology and Evolution*, 28(1):673–683.

Jukka Sirén, William P. Hanage, and Jukka Corander. 2013. Inference on population histories by approximating infinite alleles diffusion. *Journal of Molecular Biology and Evolution*, 30(2):457–468.

Sergei A. Starostin. 2005. Tower of Babel: StarLing etymological databases. http://newstar.rinet.ru/.

Lydia Steiner, Peter F Stadler, and Michael Cysouw. 2011. A pipeline for computational historical linguistics. *Language Dynamics and Change*, 1(1):89–127.

Fabian Vázquez, Xavier Castelló, and Maxi San Miguel. 2010. Agent based models of language competition: Macroscopic descriptions and order-disorder transitions. *Journal of Statistical Mechanics: Theory and Experiment*, 2010:P04007.

Stephan Vogel, Hermann Ney, and Christoph Tillmann. 1996. HMM-based word alignment in statistical translation. In *Proceedings of 16th Conference on Computational Linguistics (COLING 96)*, pages 169–174, Copenhagen, Denmark.

Hannes Wettig, Suvi Hiltunen, and Roman Yangarber. 2011. MDL-based Models for Alignment of Etymological Data. In *Proceedings of RANLP: the 8th Conference on Recent Advances in Natural Language Processing*, Hissar, Bulgaria.

Hannes Wettig, Kirill Reshetnikov, and Roman Yangarber. 2012. Using context and phonetic features in models of etymological sound change. In *Proc. EACL Workshop on Visualization of Linguistic Patterns and Uncovering Language History from Multilingual Resources*, pages 37–44, Avignon, France.

Dmitry Zelenko. 2009. Combining MDL transliteration training with discriminative modeling. In *Proceedings of the ACL-IJCNLP*, Singapore.

An incremental model of syntactic bootstrapping

Christos Christodoulopoulos[*], Dan Roth[*] and **Cynthia Fisher[†]**
[*]Department of Computer Science   [†]Department of Psychology
University of Illinois at Urbana-Champaign
{christod,danr,clfishe}@illinois.edu

Abstract

Syntactic bootstrapping is the hypothesis that learners can use the preliminary syntactic structure of a sentence to identify and characterise the meanings of novel verbs. Previous work has shown that syntactic bootstrapping can begin using only a few seed nouns (Connor et al., 2010; Connor et al., 2012). Here, we relax their key assumption: rather than training the model over the entire corpus at once (*batch mode*), we train the model incrementally, thus more realistically simulating a human learner. We also improve on the verb prediction method by incorporating the assumption that verb assignments are stable over time. We show that, given a high enough number of seed nouns (around 30), an incremental model achieves similar performance to the batch model. We also find that the number of seed nouns shown to be sufficient in the previous work is not sufficient under the more realistic incremental model. The results demonstrate that adopting more realistic assumptions about the early stages of language acquisition can provide new insights without undermining performance.

1   Introduction

An important aspect of how children acquire language is how they map lexical units and their combinations to underlying semantic representations (Gleitman, 1990). Syntactic bootstrapping is an account of this aspect of language learning. It is the hypothesis that learners can use the syntactic structure of a sentence to characterise the meanings of novel verbs. However, the problem remains of how learners first identify verbs, and

characterise the syntactic structure of sentences.

One mechanism for resolving this issue is Structure Mapping (Fisher et al., 2010), which hypothesises that, assuming an innate one-to-one mapping between nouns and semantic arguments in an utterance, children are able to use this information to first identify verbs and their arguments, and then assign semantic roles to those arguments. In this paper we provide a computational model for this account of syntactic bootstrapping. We use a system called *BabySRL* (Connor et al., 2010; Connor et al., 2012) that assigns semantic roles to arguments in an utterance – a simplified version of the Semantic Role Labeling Task (SRL; (Palmer et al., 2011)). Here, we focus on the preliminary task of identifying nouns and verbs from sentences in a corpus of child-directed speech (the Brown corpus (Brown, 1973), a subset of the CHILDES database (MacWhinney, 2000)). Previous work (Connor et al., 2010) presented a model which could identifying noun and verb clusters with minimal supervision (a few seed nouns). However, this model had two substantial limitations: the first was training was done in a *batch* mode, where the entire dataset was made available to the learner before any predictions were made; the second was that while the noun prediction was aggregated (previously identified known clusters persisted throughout the run through the data), the verb prediction was not (previously identified verb clusters had no effect on future predictions).

The current work makes two main advances on the previous work. Firstly, it addresses the batch mode limitation, adopting a more cognitively plausible approach where all sentences are given to the learner incrementally, more accurately modelling ongoing learning from child-directed speech. Secondly, it adopts an aggregated approach to verb prediction, as described in section 2.2, which capitalises on the fundamental assump-

38

Proceedings of the 7th Workshop on Cognitive Aspects of Computational Language Learning, pages 38–43,
Berlin, Germany, August 11, 2016. ©2016 Association for Computational Linguistics

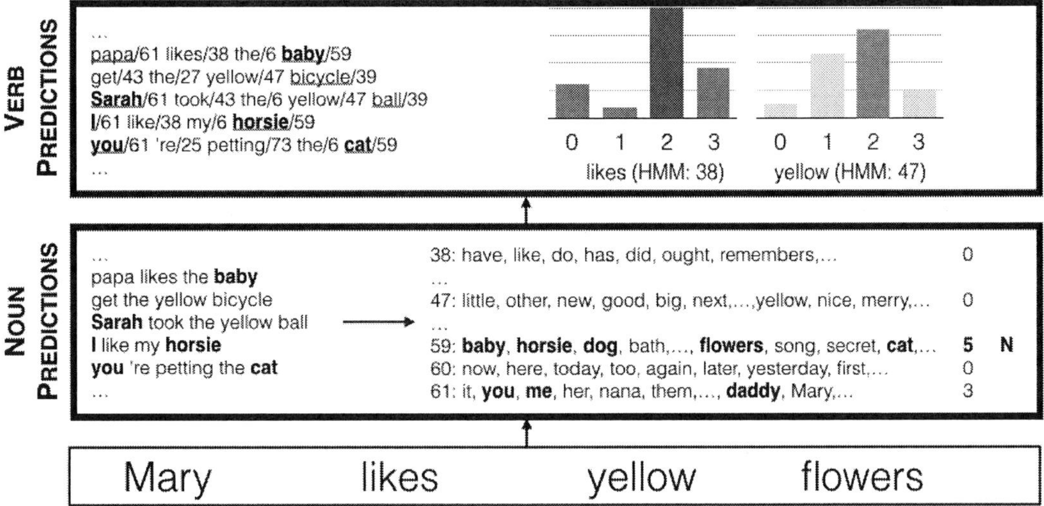

Figure 1: Illustration of the noun and verb prediction heuristics. The noun heuristic stage receives words assigned to HMM states and a list of seed nouns, and assigns the noun label to states that contain 4 or more seed nouns, assumed to be learned without syntactic help (right-hand side columns show the number of identified seeds and assignment). The verb heuristic receives a list of noun states per sentence and accumulates counts of co-occurring nouns for each of the non-noun states (right-hand side histograms). It assigns the verb label to the state with the highest probability of occurring with the number of nouns that appear in the sentence.

tion that distributional clusters will behave in a grammatically consistent fashion ("once a verb, always a verb").

2 Noun and verb prediction

Figure 1 describes the heuristics for noun and verb prediction. Firstly, we model the distributional-based word categorization with a hidden Markov model (HMM) using 80 states. We used a Variational Bayes HMM model (Beal, 2003), trained off-line over a very large corpus of child-directed speech (2.1M tokens). We then use the method described in Connor et al. (2010) to identify which of these HMM states act as arguments (nouns) and predicates (verbs). As in the original work, we also give the HMM a number of function words as identified by their part-of-speech tags in order to be clustered into separate reserved states. This represents (but does not model explicitly) the assumption that infant learners can identify function words based on a variety of cues, including linguistic context, prosody, and frequency (Gerken and McIntosh, 1993; Christophe et al., 2008; Hochmann, 2013). Note also, that the list of function words was given to the HMM during training and not during the tagging of the BabySRL cor-

pus. This means that for this corpus, the HMM is using the same distributional statistics as for the content words to decide on the function-word state membership.

2.1 Identifying nouns

As in Connor et al. (2010), we use a simple heuristic to identify noun HMM states. We assume a number of (up to 75) "seed" nouns (taken from Dale and Fenson (1996) – we chose the words that were produced by at least 50% of children under 21 months old). These words, assumed to be learned without syntactic knowledge, are recognised by the learner as verb arguments by virtue of structure-mappings one-to-one mapping assumption (Fisher et al., 2010). Using that knowledge, the learner is able to identify which HMM states contain these nouns and label them as arguments. Any state that contains 4 or more seed nouns is labelled as a noun state. We also experimented with a *dynamic* noun threshold: rather than keeping it to a fixed number (4), we used a number of functions that would dynamically increase this threshold according to the number of seed nouns presented to the learner. Experiments that increased the threshold up to 30 with linear, exponential, or logarithmic functions revealed no significant difference in results.

2.2 Identifying verbs

After running the noun heuristic, each remaining word (that does not belong to a function-word HMM state) is considered a candidate verb. For the purposes of this process, we assume that there is a single verb for each utterance. However, we use all the sentences available in the BabySRL corpus, a bare majority of which (51%) have only one verb predicate.

For the verb identification heuristic, we create a histogram of the number of times each non-noun content word (verb candidate) co-occurs with a specific number of noun arguments (shown in the top right of Figure 1). After this stage, as discussed in the Introduction, we diverge from the original model and adopt an aggregated prediction policy. The original model simply chose the "winner" of the histogram-based predictions: the candidate i with state s_i that maximized the probability of the identified number of noun arguments. For this new model, instead of assigning the verb label directly to the winner, we aggregate the predictions for each sentence into two numbers: the number of times state s_i was chosen as the the winner of the histogram-based predictions ($\#s_i(pred)$), and the overall number of times state s_i appeared in the corpus ($\#s_i(\cdot)$). From these two numbers we can calculate the probability of this state being a "stable" verb, $p(s_i(pred)) = (\#s_i(pred)/\#s_i(\cdot))$. For each sentence, we then pick the candidate whose state has the highest probability of being a stable verb. If multiple candidates have the same state and therefore the same probability, we choose the first.[1]

One of the corollaries of this experiment is that for the verb heuristic to work, the true argument structure of a verb (number of *core* arguments) has to align with the number of predicted arguments (nouns). To verify this, we looked at the number of times a verb's core arguments agree with the number of gold-standard nouns. We found that this is true for 36.3% of the sentences with a single verb (30.6% overall). This seemingly low score reflects the fact that not all arguments are single nouns: some contain no nouns, (as in the adjec-

tive argument of "looks nice"), and some contain multiple nouns, mostly in the form of conjunctions ("the boy and the girl").[2] The implication here is that if the verb heuristic was only using the count histograms as a source of information, its performance would have been mediocre. However, by excluding noun and function words states as potential arguments, the verb heuristic is able to achieve a pretty robust precision as we will see in section 4.

3 Incremental prediction

During language acquisition, children are exposed to learning data incrementally, meaning they are not exposed to all the data before having to generate their own hypotheses. To model this incremental exposure, the following changes to the original model were made.

Rather than noun prediction preceding verb prediction, in the incremental model both processes happen concurrently. When the model is exposed to the first sentence, it will identify no noun states because none of them exceed the threshold of 4 seed nouns. However, if a seed noun occurs, its appearance will be counted towards the sum of its state.

For example, in a case where the first four utterances in the corpus are as follows (HMM states are indicated by numbers following their corresponding word, function-word states are in grey and seed nouns are in bold):

(1)   a.   papa/57 wants/58 an/6 **apple**/39
        b.   get/43 the/27 red/79 **bicycle**/39
        c.   come/75 and/21 move/43 **horsie**/39
        d.   **i**/50 forgot/63 a/6 **spoon**/39
        e.   **you**/50 're/25 eating/73 the/6 broom/39

When the model reaches utterance (1-a), it recognises the seed noun 'apple', and so increments the counter for state 39. The only information available to the verb prediction module at this point is that 'apple', as a seed noun, is a potential noun. Therefore, this sentence contains two possible verbs, 'papa' and 'wants' ('a/an' has a known function-word state). Therefore, both states 57 and 58 are stored in the verb histograms as having one argument and since it appears first (see foot-

---

[1]This method could allow us to predict multiple verbs per sentence, if instead of assigning the state with the highest probability, we set a threshold over which every state is assigned the verb label.

[2]Compound nouns ("ice cream" or "fire truck") are discounted using a simple heuristic of joining contiguous noun mentions.

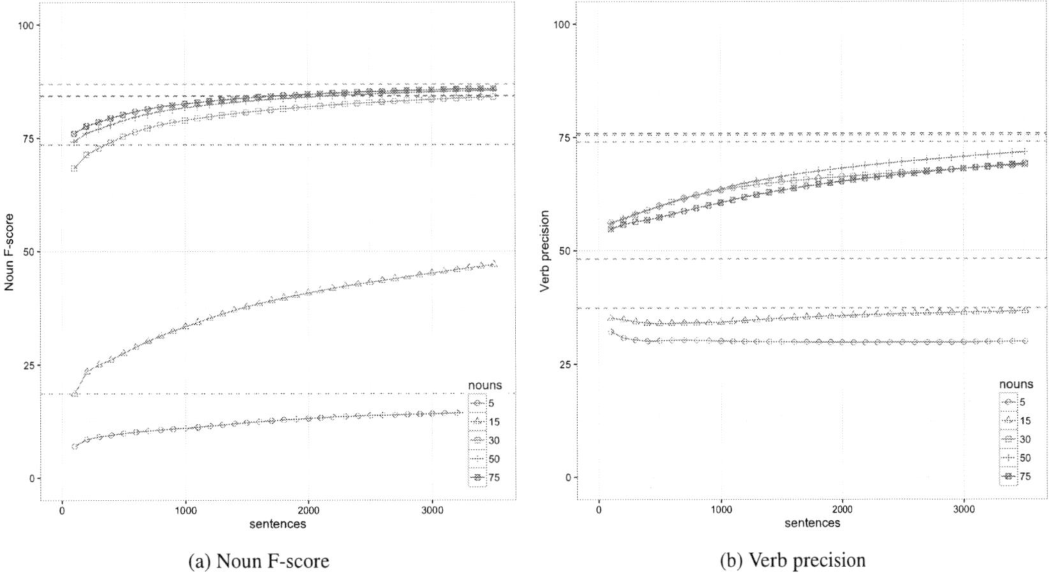

(a) Noun F-score   (b) Verb precision

Figure 2: Results from the incremental noun/verb prediction, averaged over three children from the Brown corpus (solid lines). The x axis shows the number of sentences. Colours indicate number of seed nouns. For reference, dotted lines show results from the batch mode heuristics over all sentences including those with multiple verbs, using the same verb aggregation techniques described in section 2.2. For nouns, F-score is used, since the model predicts multiple nouns per utterance. For verbs, since only one verb is predicted per utterance, precision is used as the evaluation metric.

note 1), 'papa' will be chosen as the verb.[3]

The process repeats for utterances (1-b)–(1-d), each of which contains one seed noun in state 39. When the system reaches utterance (1-e), state 39 will have attained the threshold of 4 identified nouns. Utterance (1-e) therefore contains one noun identified via this noun heuristic, 'broom', and one known seed noun, 'you', leaving 'eating' as the only allowable verb candidate, and correctly predicting the argument histogram count (2) for its state (73). Using this toy example, we can see how it will not take long for both the noun and verb heuristics to reach the prediction level of the batch mode via an incremental process.

Note that while noun and verb prediction is truly incremental, the preliminary HMM learning and state assignments happen in batch mode. This as-

sumption could be relaxed in future, since there already exist incremental models of word category assignment (Parisien et al., 2008; Fountain and Lapata, 2011). Here, as with the original work, we chose not to focus on this earlier stage of language acquisition, and instead assume that learning distributional facts about words proceeds largely independently for some time, until a few nouns are known – at which point syntax guides interpretation of the distributional classes. However, we know that category learning itself is influenced by syntactic properties (Christodoulopoulos et al., 2012). As such, in future work we plan to integrate the syntactic category learning with the verb and noun prediction stage to improve the accuracy of both.

4 Results and Discussion

We now present the results of the two main advances over the previous work of Connor et al. (2010): the incremental version of the verb and noun heuristics, and the aggregated predictions for the verb heuristic.

Figure 2 shows the results from the two tasks of noun and verb prediction averaged over three chil-

---

[3]The storing of both states 57 and 58 as potential one-argument verbs in the example may seem to conflict with the assumption that there is only one verb per sentence. It is true that at this stage, the model will lose information relevant to the true number of arguments of each verb, since potential arguments may be wrongly identified as verb candidates. However, the statistical stability of verb argument-taking behaviour, as well as the incrementally improving noun heuristic, leads to these early errors being corrected. In addition, this approach leaves space for a future version of this model where multiple verbs per sentence can be predicted.

41

dren, as well as the results of the original batch version from Connor et al. (2010). It is worth noting that the three children in the Brown corpus had different numbers of sentences that came from different age ranges. As such, the average trajectories mask substantial individual differences. There are two main findings: 1) the incremental scores for each number of seed nouns slowly converge to those of the batch mode; 2) similar to the original study, there is a plateau for both noun and verb prediction scores around 30 seed nouns.

For the noun prediction, we can see that the number of seed nouns it takes to reach comparable performance is slightly higher than in the batch mode model. For instance, with 15 seed nouns, the incremental prediction achieves a score of 47.1%, whereas the batch mode achieves a score of 73.6%. This is important, because it shows that the number of seed nouns the batch mode suggested was sufficient is not sufficient under a more realistic incremental model. Interestingly, this difference is not as pronounced for the verb prediction scores. The reason for this is that by aggregating over the histogram-based predictions, we can recover from more noise coming from the noun assignment. We also replicated the original (non-aggregated) verb heuristic from Connor et al. (2010). The results follow similar trends, although the absolute numbers are lower. This is verified our intuition that the grammatical 'meaning' of HMM states is indeed stable.

This work also raises a more general point about computational models of language learning. Real human learners not only have limited resources such as memory and processing power, but also are exposed to training instances incrementally and only once. Related work in the field of computer vision tries to mimic these learning conditions ("one-shot learning", Fei-Fei et al. (2006)), but this approach has not yet attracted much attention in the field of computational modeling of language acquisition.[4] We present these results as a preliminary step in this direction, showing that we can still attain good performance even while acknowledging these limitations, and that this can give us more insights into what exactly human learners require to support acquisition.

---

[4]A notable exception is the work on incremental word category acquisition mentioned above (Parisien et al., 2008; Fountain and Lapata, 2011).

5 Conclusion

In this paper, we presented an incremental version of the syntactic bootstrapping model of Connor et al. (2010), with the additional innovation of aggregating over verb predictions – the latter representing the fundamental assumption that the tagging of HMM states with grammatical category "meaning" is stable ("once a verb, always a verb"). We showed that given a high enough number of seed nouns, an incremental model can achieve similar performance within around 2000 sentences for noun predictions and 3000 sentences for verb predictions. Importantly, the results also show that the number of seed nouns shown to be sufficient in the previous work is not sufficient under a more realistic model where the learner encounters data incrementally. More broadly, we demonstrate that adopting more realistic assumptions about the early stages of language acquisition can tell us more about what learners require to bootstrap the acquisition of syntactic categories while maintaining high performance.

Acknowledgments

The authors would like to thank the anonymous reviewers for their suggestions. Many thanks also to Catriona Silvey for her help with the manuscript. This research is supported by NIH grant R01-HD054448-07.

References

Matthew James Beal. 2003. *Variational algorithms for approximate Bayesian inference*. Ph.D. thesis, University of London.

Roger Brown. 1973. *A first language: The early stages*. Harvard U. Press.

Christos Christodoulopoulos, Sharon Goldwater, and Mark Steedman. 2012. Turning the pipeline into a loop: Iterated unsupervised dependency parsing and pos induction. In *Proceedings of the NAACL-HLT Workshop on the Induction of Linguistic Structure*, pages 96–99, June.

Anne Christophe, Séverine Millotte, Savita Bernal, and Jeffrey Lidz. 2008. Bootstrapping lexical and syntactic acquisition. *Language and speech*, 51(1-2):61–75.

Michael Connor, Yael Gertner, Cynthia Fisher, and Dan Roth. 2010. Starting from Scratch in Semantic Role Labeling. In *Proceedings of the 48th Annual Meeting of the Association for Computational Linguistics*, Uppsala, Sweden, jul. Association for Computational Linguistics.

Michael Connor, Cynthia Fisher, and Dan Roth. 2012. Starting from scratch in semantic role labeling: Early indirect supervision. In A. Alishahi, T. Poibeau, and A. Korhonen, editors, *Cognitive Aspects of Computational Language Acquisition*. Springer.

Philip S. Dale and Larry Fenson. 1996. Lexical development norms for young children. *Behavior Research Methods, Instruments, & Computers*, 28(1):125–127.

Li Fei-Fei, Rob Fergus, and Pietro Perona. 2006. One-shot learning of object categories. *Pattern Analysis and Machine Intelligence, IEEE Transactions on*, 28(4):594–611.

Cynthia Fisher, Yael Gertner, Rose M Scott, and Sylvia Yuan. 2010. Syntactic bootstrapping. *Wiley Interdisciplinary Reviews: Cognitive Science*, 1(2):143–149, mar.

Trevor Fountain and Mirella Lapata. 2011. Incremental models of natural language category acquisition. In *Proceedings of the 32st Annual Conference of the Cognitive Science Society*.

LouAnn Gerken and Bonnie J McIntosh. 1993. Interplay of function morphemes and prosody in early language. *Developmental psychology*, 29(3):448.

Lila Gleitman. 1990. The Structural Sources of Verb Meanings. *Language Acquisition*, 1(1):3–55, jan.

Jean-Rémy Hochmann. 2013. Word frequency, function words and the second gavagai problem. *Cognition*, 128(1):13–25, jul.

Brian MacWhinney. 2000. *The CHILDES project: The database*, volume 2. Psychology Press.

Martha Palmer, Daniel Gildea, and Nianwen Xue. 2011. *Semantic Role Labeling*. Morgan & Claypool Publishers, feb.

Christopher Parisien, Afsaneh Fazly, and Suzanne Stevenson. 2008. An incremental bayesian model for learning syntactic categories. In *Proceedings of the Twelfth Conference on Computational Natural Language Learning*, pages 89–96. Association for Computational Linguistics.

Longitudinal Studies of Variation Sets in Child-directed Speech

Mats Wirén, Kristina Nilsson Björkenstam, Gintarė Grigonytė and Elisabet Eir Cortes
Department of Linguistics
Stockholm University
SE-106 91 Stockholm, Sweden
{mats.wiren, kristina.nilsson, gintare, elisabet.cortes}@ling.su.se

Abstract

One of the characteristics of child-directed speech is its high degree of repetitiousness. Sequences of repetitious utterances with a constant intention, *variation sets*, have been shown to be correlated with children's language acquisition. To obtain a baseline for the occurrences of variation sets in Swedish, we annotate 18 parent–child dyads using a generalised definition according to which the varying form may pertain not just to the wording but also to prosody and/or non-verbal cues. To facilitate further empirical investigation, we introduce a surface algorithm for automatic extraction of variation sets which is easily replicable and language-independent. We evaluate the algorithm on the Swedish gold standard, and use it for extracting variation sets in Croatian, English and Russian. We show that the proportion of variation sets in child-directed speech decreases consistently as a function of children's age across Swedish, Croatian, English and Russian.

1 Introduction

1.1 Background and motivation

Child-directed speech has many characteristics that set it apart from adult-directed language, such as shorter utterances, lower speech rate, fewer disfluencies, lower syntactic complexity, greater modulation of F_0 and high repetitiousness (Broen, 1972). Here is an example of the latter property from our data:[1]

> You can put the animals there.
> You can take the pig and the cat and put
>   them there.
> Can you put them there?
> Good.
> Can you put the pig there too?

Sequences of such (partial) self-repetitions with a constant intention have been called *variation sets*, and have been shown to account for a large proportion of the language that children hear (Küntay and Slobin, 1996; Clark., 2009, p. 37).[2]

Why does this phenomenon occur? To some extent, repetitiousness may serve simply to capture and maintain the child's attention, but our intuitions tell us that it is likely to also facilitate language learning for infants. For example, it may allow for effective segmentation of phonetic material (Bard and Anderson, 1983), and it has been shown to be a predictor of syntax growth (Hoff-Ginsberg, 1986; Hoff-Ginsberg, 1990; Waterfall, 2006). In a similar vein, investigating social and attentional cues in word learning, Frank et al. (2012), point out that the temporal proximity and continuity of repetitious language create supportive contexts where partial understanding of individual utterances can lead to fuller understanding.[3]

But variation sets have also been shown to benefit artificial language learning. In an experiment on this, Onnis et al. (2008) showed that adults exposed to input with varation sets performed better in phrase segmentation and phrase-boundary judgement tasks than a control group who heard

---

[1]Translation of utterances from the MINGLE-3 corpus (Björkenstam and Wirén, 2014) with parental speech to a child aged 1;3 (compare Section 3).

[2]"Variation set" is actually a misnomer, since the idea is that the order of individual utterances is important.

[3]It is also interesting to note that child-directed signing shares many characteristics of child-directed speech, such as prosodic exaggeration, lexical and syntactic simplification, and repetition (Masataka, 2000), and these shared characteristics include variation sets (Hoiting and Slobin, 2002).

Proceedings of the 7th Workshop on Cognitive Aspects of Computational Language Learning, pages 44–52,
Berlin, Germany, August 11, 2016. ©2016 Association for Computational Linguistics

the same input in scrambled order without variation sets. They note that "[f]rom a computational standpoint, the key characteristic of variation sets is that local mechanisms of alignment and comparison allow even memory-limited learners to discover structure that they would otherwise miss" (Onnis et al., 2008, p. 424).

1.2 Related work

Early studies of child-directed language dealing with partial and exact repetition include Broen (1972), Snow (1972), Kaye (1980) and Hoff-Ginsberg (1986; 1990). For example, Broen (*ibid.*, p. 29, 43) tracked "clusters of sequential sentences" where "the meaning remains constant". Snow (*ibid.*) found more partial and exact repetitions to 2-year olds than to 10-year olds.

Küntay and Slobin (1996) introduced the term "variation set", by which they meant a contiguous sequence of repetitions with varying form but constant intention. They pointed out that the core of a variation set (and the main vehicle for expressing the intention) is almost always a verb, with optionally expressed arguments. (In the above example from the MINGLE-3 corpus, this verb would be "put".) The possible variations were taken to be "(1) lexical substitution and rephrasing, (2) addition and deletion of specific referential terms, and (3) reordering of constituents" (Küntay and Slobin, 2002, p. 6). Their definition did not include exact repetitions, however. Furthermore, it appears that in order for a new utterance to be considered a member of a existing variation set, the new utterance has to satisfy the above conditions for *all* of the previous utterances taken to be in the set.

Küntay and Slobin's study was based on transcripts of everyday interaction between a Turkish-speaking mother and her child over a seven-month period, during which the child was between 1;8 and 2;3 years. The finding was that 21% of the utterances occurred within variation sets, and that these sets were positively associated with children's acquisition of specific verbs. A follow-up study of transcripts of another Turkish-speaking mother and a child (at age 1;3 and 2;0 years) showed how the communicative functions of the variation sets changed as a function of age (Küntay and Slobin, 2002).

Waterfall (2006) provided the first longitudinal study of variation sets in English, based on 12 mother–child dyads with children between 1;2 and 2;6 years. Waterfall's (2006, p. 21) definition of variation set is somewhat different from Küntay and Slobin's, though it is not clear what effect that has in practice. Basically, she defines a variation set as a sequence of utterances that belongs to the same conversational turn, that relates to the same event or situation, that "have similar or related meanings", and shares at least one noun or verb. Again, it appears that these conditions should hold between all utterances within the set, and like Küntay and Slobin, she did not include exact repetitions. Also, she allowed up to four non-related intervening utterances in a variation set. Waterfall found that children's production of nominal and verbal structures was correlated with peaks in the parents' use of that structure in variation sets. She also found a moderate decrease in the proportion of utterances that are part of variation sets as a function of age, from 17% at 1;2 years to 12% at 2;6 years.

Attempts at automatic extraction of variation sets naturally focus on form rather than function. Brodsky et al. (2007) suggest a simple definition of a variation set as a sequence of utterances where each successive pair of utterances has a lexical overlap of at least one element, excluding words on a stoplist (which includes high-frequency words). Variation sets are thus extracted by comparing pairs of successive utterances for repeated words, resulting in sets with at least one non-stoplisted word in common. Using an automated procedure of this kind, Brodsky et al. obtain a proportion of 21.5% of the *words* in Waterfall's (2006) corpus occurring in variation sets, and 18.3% of the words in the English CHILDES collection (MacWhinney, 2000). Similar studies have been performed by Onnis et al. (2008) and Waterfall et al. (2010). For example, when Onnis et al. used an automated procedure based on Waterfall's (2006) criteria on the Lara corpus from CHILDES (involving one child between 1;9 and 3;3 years), they obtained a proportion of 27,9% of the utterances being inside variation sets.

1.3 The problem

For the purpose of this work, we assume that variation sets play a role in language learning for infants, but we are agnostic as to the precise nature of this role. Rather, the aim is to investigate the longitudinal behaviour of variation sets using a definition which subsumes earlier work but where the repetitiousness may also be, on the one hand, semantic (with no or very little surface repetition) and, on the other hand, prosodic or non-verbal (while displaying exact repetition). To obtain a baseline for the behaviour of this phenomenon in Swedish, we develop a gold standard for variation sets. To facilitate further empirical investigation, we introduce a surface algorithm which we evaluate on the gold standard and apply to Croatian, English and Russian.

2 Criteria for variation sets

2.1 Basic criteria

A starting-point for our work is Küntay and Slobin's (1996; 2002) definition, which takes variation sets to be sequences of utterances with the same communicative intention but with small differences in form. Basically, our definition subsumes Küntay and Slobin's, but we extend it in certain ways. First, along with Brodsky et al. (2007), we extract variation sets (whether manually in the gold standard or automatically using the algorithm) by comparing successive pairs of utterances: first–second, second–third, etc. Also, up to two intervening utterances (such as interjections) by the parent are allowed any time in a sequence (similarly to Snow (1972, p. 251) and Brodsky et al. (2007)). Furthermore, we allow for verbal input from the child within variation sets. The rationale for this is that our data covers the ages 0;7–2;9 years (see Section 3), and especially in the early dyads the children are still learning to take turns. As for constant intention, we make one exception from this, following Küntay and Slobin (2002): we include question–answer sequences where the parent provides both the question and the answer in variation sets.

2.2 Surface and semantic repetitiousness

A difference compared to previous work that we are aware of is that we aim at capturing a continuous scale of surface and semantic repetitiousness, where, at one extreme, the repetitiousness may be purely semantic without any surface similarity at all. Here is an example of this from our data, with approximate translations:

> Titta här då!
> (But look here!)
> Har du sett vilka tjusiga byxor?

(Have you seen the fancy pants?)
Kolla!
(Look!)

The intention in each of these utterances is to make the child look at the pants, but there is no overlap whatsoever in form between the utterances.

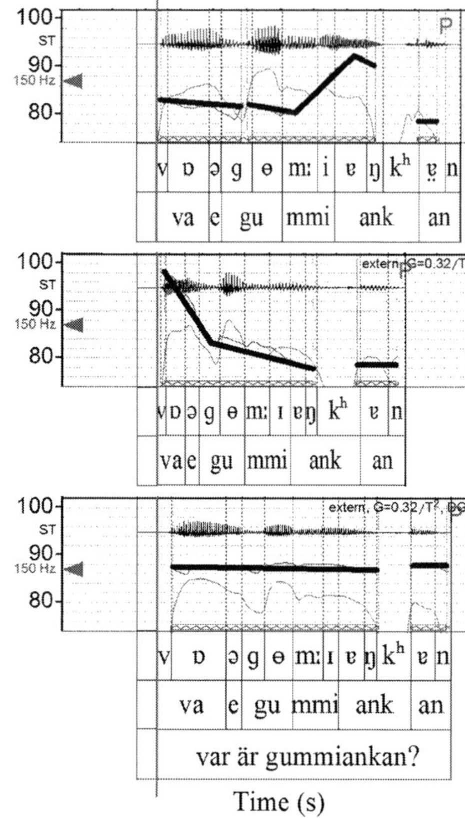

Figure 1: Phonetic and prosodic analysis of a repetition of the Swedish phrase "Var är gummiankan?" ("Where is the rubber duck?"), uttered by a male speaker. The utterances are ordered with the first utterance on top. The y-axis represents frequency (semitones) and the x-axis represents time (seconds). Black thick horizontal lines show stylised intonation based on tonal perception.

2.3 Multimodal variation

Contrary to many previous studies of variation sets (Küntay and Slobin, 1996; Küntay and Slobin, 2002; Waterfall, 2006), we include exact (verbatim) repetitions in our definition of variation sets. This is motivated by the result of a study that we made of three dyads in the multimodally annotated MINGLE-3 corpus (see Section 3). Whenever word-for-word repetition occurred in the written transcript of the three dyads, we found consistent patterns of prosodic variation in the parents' speech, involving pitch, timing and/or stress, and typically also variation of their non-verbal cues, involving eye gaze direction, deictic gestures or object manipulation.

Figure 1 shows a phonetic and prosodic analysis of a variation set from our data with three exact repetitions of the Swedish utterance "Var är gummiankan?" ("Where is the rubber duck?").[4] The vertical line indicates time-synchronized starts of the repetitions. In the analysis window for each repetition, a black thick horizontal line shows stylized intonation based on tonal perception (perceived pitch). A downwards tilted line means falling intonation (from brighter to deeper voice), upwards tilted means rising intonation. In the background, the waveform and intensity (thin line) can be seen. The annotation rows beneath each repetition contains phonetic transcription in IPA (top row) and syllable segmentation (second row). The third row at the bottom contains an orthographic annotation.[5]

Here, the first utterance (shown at the top of the figure) initially displays relatively flat intonation, and then rising intonation with a peak on the first syllable in the noun "ankan" ("duck"), with a fall on the last syllable. In contrast, the second utterance has shorter duration and falling intonation throughout. Finally, the third utterance has completely flat intonation, with duration similar to the first utterance but with a prolongation of the first syllable, corresponding to the adverb "var" ("where").

Although this is just a small study, the fact that variation is here being systematically manifested through prosody and/or non-verbal cues when the wording is constant fits well with our general impression of exact repetitions. It is because of this multimodal variation that we include verbatim repetitions in variation sets.

3   Data

Our data consists of transcripts of Swedish child-directed speech from the MINGLE-3 corpus (Björkenstam and Wirén, 2014), consisting of 18 longitudinal dyads with three children (two girls, one boy) recorded between the ages of 7 and 33 months with six dyads per child, all of which is multimodally annotated. The complete duration of the 18 dyads is 7:29 hours (mean duration 24:58 minutes). The video and audio recordings were made from naturalistic parent–child interaction in a recording studio at the Phonetics Laboratory at Stockholm University (Lacerda, 2009). The children were interacting alternately with their mothers (10 dyads) and fathers (8 dyads). The scenario was free play.[6] The ELAN annotation tool (Wittenburg et al., 2006) was used for transcription of parent and child utterances, as well as annotation of eye gaze, deictic gestures and object manipulation (Björkenstam and Wirén, 2014). The transcripts have been automatically annotated with part-of-speech and morphosyntactic tags using Stagger (Östling, 2013), followed by manual correction.

4   Creating a gold standard

The manual annotation of variation sets started with analysis of four dyads, based on a guideline according to the criteria in Section 2. The same criteria were applied throughout all age groups. The annotations were made in ELAN, using timelines to code the extensions of variations sets across utterances, and taking into account both verbal and non-verbal input from parent and child from transcriptions, audio and video.

Each of the four dyads was annotated by two coders independently. The resulting annotations were merged, and a third annotator marked cases of disagreement. This resulted in an interannotator agreement (measured as set overlap between annotators) of 78%. The remaining 14 dyads were annotated by one annotator. During this phase, a classification of communicative intention based on the Inventory of Communicative Acts-Abridged (Ninio et al., 1994) was added. This classification was evaluated by comparing four representative dyads annotated by three independent annotators, resulting in a Fleiss's kappa of 0.63.

---

[4]The examples in this section are from the MINGLE-3 corpus (Björkenstam and Wirén, 2014), with approximate English translations.

[5]The intonation analyses were done in Prosogram (Mertens, 2004), and the figures were compiled from Prosogram and Praat (Boersma, 2001).

[6]Some of the data (transcripts and audio) is available through the Swedish section of CHILDES as the Lacerda files (MacWhinney, 2000).

Table 1: Results of the longitudinal study of Swedish variation sets (also used as gold standard in Table 3). The third row shows the proportions of child-directed utterances that are in variation sets. Each figure is obtained by first calculating the proportion per dyad and then averaging the proportions over all dyads in the respective age group. Boldface indicates statistically significant difference to boldfaced neighbour (z-test of sample proportions; respectively, $z = 8$, $p < 0.0001$, $z = 2.3$, $p < 0.02$, $z = 8.2$, $p < 0.0001$, two-tailed). The fourth row shows the proportions of exact repetitions within variation sets. Each figure is obtained by first calculating the proportion per variation set and averaging over the dyad, then averaging over all dyads in the respective age group.

Longitudinal study of Swedish variation sets	**Group 1** 0;7–0;9	**Group 2** 1;0–1;2	**Group 3** 1;4–1;7	**Group 4** 2;3–2;9
Number of dyads	5	5	5	3
Number of child-directed utterances	1032	1421	1492	724
Proportion of utterances that are in variation sets	**50%**	**34%**	**30%**	**14%**
Proportion of exact repetitions in variation sets	24%	16%	13%	10%

5 Results: Gold standard variation sets

In order to obtain a baseline for how the proportion of utterances that are in variation sets varied as a function of age of the children, we grouped the dyads according to child age in the following four data sets:

Age group 1: 0;7–0;9 (7–9 months)
Age group 2: 1;0–1;2 (12–14 months)
Age group 3: 1;4–1;7 (16–19 months)
Age group 4: 2;3–2;9 (27–33 months)

As shown in Table 1, our gold standard displayed a consistent decrease in the proportion of utterances in variation sets over time, from 50% for age group 1 to 14% for group 4. The proportion of verbatim repetitions in variation sets also decreased, from 24% for age group 1 to 10% for group 4.

6 Automatic extraction of variation sets

The method that we use for extracting variation sets is deliberately surface-based to allow us to determine how far this can bring us relative to our gold standard, which is based on both surface and semantic criteria. As mentioned above, the algorithm performs a stepwise comparison of pairs of successive utterances. The criterion for including two successive utterances in a variation set is that the difference between them (regarded as strings) does not fall below a certain similarity threshold. Additionally, following Brodsky et al. (2007) and others, we allow for sequences of maximally two intervening dissimilar utterances that do not obey this condition.

For string comparison, we used Ratcliff–Obershelp pattern recognition (Black, 2004) as implemented in the Python module `difflib`.[7] We refer to the variation-set extraction algorithm using this as "difflib ratio", DLR.[8] When comparing two strings, the matcher returns a value between 0 and 1. A value of 1 corresponds to an exact repetition, and 0 corresponds to two utterances without any overlap of words. By using this value as a parameter, we can obtain a threshold for the desired degree of similarity. The threshold can either be selected arbitrarily, or learned from evaluation against the gold standard variation sets. When evaluated against the gold standard, the optimal similarity threshold was 0.55 (see Figure 2).

We experimented with including information from the part-of-speech tagging of the transcripts (see Section 3) in such a way that the pair of strings compared consisted of both the words and their part-of-speech tags. Our intuition was that this might give us a more refined analysis, for example, by distinguishing cases of homonymy. This version of the algorithm turned out not to improve performance, however (see Figure 2), and was therefore dropped.

---

[7] `https://docs.python.org/2/library/difflib.html#module-difflib`.

[8] We also experimented with another standard technique for calculating string similarity, namely, edit distance, also known as Levenshtein distance (Levenshtein, 1966). In the end we found DLR to perform slightly better relative to the gold standard, however.

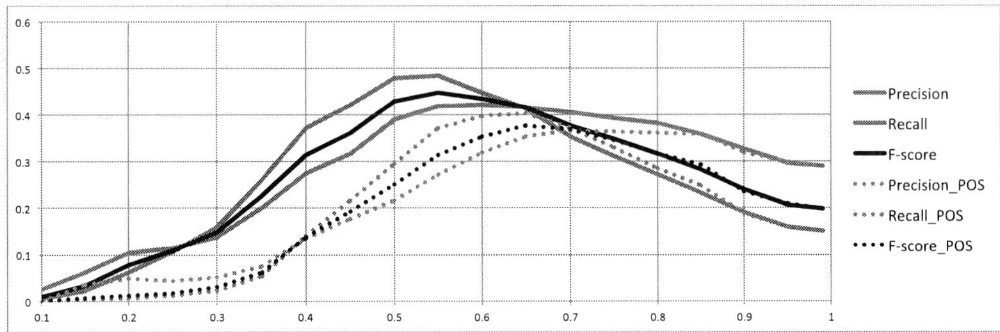

Figure 2: Results of strict matching with the DLR similarity measure on raw (solid lines) and part-of-speech tagged data (dotted lines). Similarity level thresholds on x-axis; precision, recall and F-score on y-axis.

Table 2: Example variation set from the gold standard (utterance 3–4) and utterances exrqcted by the algorithm (utterance 1–4).

Example utterances	Member of gold set	Extracted by algorithm
1. Ska vi lägga ner nånting i i väskan då? (Are we going to put something in in the bag then?)	–	Yes
2. Va? (Huh?)	–	Yes
3. Ska du lägga ner kossan i väskan kanske? (Are you going to put down the cow in the bag maybe?)	Yes	Yes
4. Ska vi lägga ner kossan? (Are we going to put down the cow?)	Yes	Yes

7 Results: Automated extraction

7.1 Evaluation on Swedish gold standard

We evaluated the algorithm against the gold standard variation sets using two kinds of metrics, which we refer to as *strict* and *fuzzy* matching. Strict matching requires exact matching on the utterance level of the extracted variation set and the corresponding gold standard set, whereas fuzzy matching allows for partial overlaps of the extracted variation set and the gold standard set. In the example in Table 2, only utterance 3 and 4 are members of the gold standard variation set, whereas the algorithm extracts utterances 1–4. Hence, the strict matching metric treats this extracted set as a false positive, whereas the fuzzy matching metric treats it as a true positive. As for fuzzy matching, we need a way of calculating precision for different degrees of overlaps with the gold set. The measure we have adopted for this purpose is *mean average precision* (MAP), see

Croft et al. (2009, p. 313).

Table 3 summarizes the results of extraction of variation sets relative to the gold standard according to the strict and fuzzy metric. Strict F-score reaches 0.56 and fuzzy F-score reaches 0.82 for age group 1, but F-scores gradually decrease with increasing age. Apparently, the variation displayed in the parents' speech becomes less amenable to surface methods as the children grow older. An indirect sign of this increased complexity in variation sets is that the proportion of exact repetitions decreases as the children grow older, as shown in Table 1.

7.2 Extraction of variation sets in Croatian, English and Russian

To investigate the behaviour of variation sets in other languages, we ran the algorithm with lon-

Table 3: Evaluation of the algorithm for automatic variation-set extraction against the Swedish gold standard per age group.

String matching relative to gold standard	Group 1 0;7–0;9	Group 2 1;0–1;2	Group 3 1;4–1;7	Group 4 2;3–2;9
Strict precision	0.539	0.406	0.351	0.217
Strict recall	0.581	0.406	0.446	0.333
Strict *F*-score	**0.559**	**0.406**	**0.392**	**0.262**
Fuzzy precision	0.774	0.627	0.505	0.324
Fuzzy recall	0.877	0.763	0.743	0.615
Fuzzy *F*-score	**0.822**	**0.689**	**0.601**	**0.425**

Table 4: Results of the algorithm for automatic variation-set extraction applied to Croatian, English and Russian child-directed utterances from CHILDES. The rows show the number of utterances in each age group, the average proportion of utterances that are in variation sets, and the average proportion of exact repetitions in the variation sets, with figures having being calculated in the same way as in Table 1.

Language	Features of the data set	Group 1 0;7–0;9	Group 2 1;0–1;2	Group 3 1;4–1;7	Group 4 2;3–2;9
Croatian Kovacevic	Total number of utterances	39	217	408	(no data)
	Utterances in variation sets	85%	54%	50%	–
	Exact repetitions in variation sets	0.0%	8.5%	4.9%	–
English (UK) Lara	Total number of utterances	(no data)	(no data)	926	391
	Utterances in variation sets	–	–	54%	44%
	Exact repetitions in variation sets	–	–	7.8%	6.9%
Russian Protassova	Total number of utterances	(no data)	(no data)	1088	545
	Utterances in variation sets	–	–	35%	24%
	Exact repetitions in variation sets	–	–	6.3%	4.6%

gitudinal corpora in Croatian,[9] English[10] and Russian from CHILDES (MacWhinney, 2000).[11] Although it was not possible to find a perfect correspondance with the age groups for Swedish, Table 4 shows how the selection of languages and transcripts from CHILDES partly matches the Swedish data. As shown in Table 4, both the proportion of variation sets and the proportion of exact repetitions as far, as can be seen, decrease consistently for Croatian, English and Russian.

8   Discussion

In our study of the Swedish gold standard, we obtained statistically significant decreases in the proportion of utterances within variation sets as a function of age between all age groups, from 50% for age group 1 to 14% for age group 4 (see Table 1). These differences were also more consistent than in Waterfall (2006), who obtained an overall decrease from 17% for 1;2 years to 12% for 2;6 years (*ibid.*, p. 125). Waterfall's age span was shorter than ours,[12] but its decrease was still less pronounced within the comparable age interval. It is also interesting to see that we obtained the largest proportion of variation sets for the youngest age group (0;7–0;9 years), which was not covered by Waterfall.

The fact that we see larger age-related differences in our data does not seem to be attributable to the inclusion of exact repetitions in our variation sets, judging from the proportiones of these in Table 1. In any case, and as argued in Section 2, the reason for extending the definition of variation sets in this way is motivated by an in-

[9]Kovacevic: Vjeran, files 20 (0;10 years) 23 (1;2 years), 33 (1;7 years).

[10]Lara, files 1-09-13 (1;9 years), 2-06-00 (2;6 years).

[11]Protassova: Varv, files 01 (1;6 years), 04 (1;10 years), 06 (2;4 years).

[12]Waterfall's age group 1;2 roughly matches our group 2, 1;6 and 1;8 roughly match our group 3, and 2;2 and 2;6 roughly match our group 4. Our results for age group 1 are new compared to previous studies, however.

depth analysis of a subset of these utterances in our multimodally annotated corpus. We conjecture that when an utterance is repeated verbatim, there is instead multimodal variation that increases the information and helps the child learn from the utterance. As far as we know, our longitudinal figures on proportions of exact repetitions are also the first that have been reported.

Our automatic algorithm for variation set extraction is deliberately surface-based in order to test how far this kind of method can bring us. An independent advantage is that it is easily replicable since it is based on a standard library for string comparison. The algorithm reaches a fuzzy F-score of up to 0.82 (strict: up to 0.56) relative to the Swedish gold standard in spite of only using criteria related to form. The F-score drops as a function of age, however (see Table 3); we conjecture that this is due to the relation between form and intention becoming less transparent with increased age. That is, as the child develops and learns more language, the parents' variation gets more complex. One way of handling this complexity would be by generalizing the algorithm to recognize intention.

Since the algorithm only uses form-based criteria, it is in principle also language-independent. We obtain consistent decreases of the proportions of utterances in variation sets also when we apply the algorithm to Croatian, English and Russian corpora of child-directed language (see Table 4). Although in this case we have no evaluations, it is interesting to see that the behaviour corresponds to what we expected.

9 Conclusion

We have investigated the longitudinal behaviour of variation sets in child-directed speech according to a generalised definition. Variation sets appear to function as a device for effective communication and learning with young children: the speaker repeats the same content while varying the wording, prosody and/or non-verbal cues in order to maximise the chance of comprehension. With increasing age and language comprehension, there is less need for such repetitiousness.

Our study of Swedish covered a larger age span and displayed a more consistent decrease than Waterfall's (2006) study of American English. Our automatic algorithm seems to usefully approximate manual extraction of variation sets at least for lower age groups, and an advantage is that the algorithm is easily replicable. Applications of the algorithm to Croatian, English and Russian displayed similar decreases in the proportions of utterances in variation sets as a function of ages. We also found that the proportions of exact repetitions are similarly decreasing as a function of age for all languages, and we have demonstrated how multimodal cues seem to provide other dimensions of variation in these utterances.

Acknowledgements

This research is part of the project "Modelling the emergence of linguistic structures in early childhood", funded by the Swedish Research Council as 2011-675-86010-31. We would like to thank Lisa Tengstrand and Claudia Eklås Tejman for annotation work, and Annika Otsa for extracting and preparing the CHILDES data. Finally, we would like to thank the three anonymous reviewers for valuable comments.

References

Ellen Gurman Bard and Anne H. Anderson. 1983. The unintelligibility of speech to children. *Journal of Child Language*, 10(2):265–292.

Kristina Nilsson Björkenstam and Mats Wirén. 2014. Multimodal annotation of synchrony in parent-child interaction. In *Proceedings of The 10th Workshop on Multimodal Corpora: Combining applied and basic research targets, 2014*, Reykjavik, Iceland, May. ELRA.

Paul E Black. 2004. Ratcliff/obershelp pattern recognition. *Dictionary of Algorithms and Data Structures*, 17.

Paul Boersma. 2001. Praat, a system for doing phonetics by computer. *Glot International*, 5(9/10):341–345.

Peter Brodsky, Heidi R. Waterfall, and Shimon Edelman. 2007. Characterizing motherese: On the computational structure of child-directed language. In *Proc. 29th Cognitive Science Society Conference*, Nashville, TN.

Patricia A. Broen. 1972. *The verbal environment of the language-learning child*. ASHA Monographs Number 17, American Speech and Hearing Association. Washington D.C.

Eve V. Clark. 2009. *First Language Acquisition*. Cambridge University Press, Cambridge, UK.

W. Bruce Croft, Donald Metzler, and Trevor Strohman. 2009. *Search Engines: Information Retrieval in Practice*. Addison-Wesley Publishing Company, USA.

Michael C. Frank, Joshua B. Tenenbaum, and Anne Fernald. 2012. Social and discourse contributions to the determination of reference in cross-situational learning. *Language Learning and Development*, 00:1–24.

Erika Hoff-Ginsberg. 1986. Function and structure in maternal speech: Their relation to the child's development of syntax. *Developmental Psychology*, 22(3):155–163.

Erika Hoff-Ginsberg. 1990. Maternal speech and the child's development of syntax: a further look. *Journal of Child Language*, 17:85–99.

Nini Hoiting and Dan I. Slobin. 2002. What a deaf child needs to see: Advantages of a natural sign language over a sign system. In R. Schulmeister and H. Reinitzer, editors, *Progress in sign language research. In honor of Siegmund Prillwitz/Fortschritte in der Gebärdensprachforschung. Festschrift für Siegmund Prillwitz*, pages 268–277. Signum, Hamburg.

Kenneth Kaye. 1980. Why we don't talk 'baby talk' to babies. *Journal of Child Language*, 7:489–507.

Aylin C. Küntay and Dan I. Slobin. 1996. Listening to a turkish mother: Some puzzles for acquisition. In *Social Interaction, Social Context, and Language. Essays in the Honor of Susan Ervin-Tripp*, pages 265–286. Lawrence Erlbaum, Mahwah, NJ.

Aylin C. Küntay and Dan I. Slobin. 2002. Putting interaction back into child language: Examples from Turkish. *Psychology of Language and Communication*, 6:5–14.

Francisco Lacerda. 2009. On the emergence of early linguistic functions: A biological and interactional perspective. In K. Alter, M. Horne, M. Lindgren, M. Roll, and J. von Koss Torkildsen, editors, *Brain Talk: Discourse with and in the brain*, pages 207–230. Media-Tryck, Lund, Sweden.

Vladimir I. Levenshtein. 1966. Binary codes capable of correcting deletions, insertions, and reversals. In *Soviet physics doklady*, volume 10, pages 707–710.

Brian MacWhinney. 2000. *The CHILDES Project: Tools for analyzing talk.* Lawrence Erlbaum Associates, Mahwah, NJ, 3 edition.

Nobuo Masataka. 2000. The role of modality and input in the earliest stages of language acquisition: Studies of japanese sign language. In C. Chamberlain, J. P. Morford, and R. I. Mayberry, editors, *Language acquisition by eye*, pages 3–24. Erlbaum, Hillsdale, NJ.

Piet Mertens. 2004. The prosogram: Semi-automatic transcription of prosody based on a tonal perception model. In *Proceedings of Speech Prosody 2004*, pages 549–552, Nara, Japan.

Anat Ninio, Catherine E. Snow, Barbara A. Pan, and Pamela R. Rollins. 1994. Classifying communicative acts in children's interactions. *Journal of Communicative Disorders*, 27:157–187.

Luca Onnis, Heidi R. Waterfall, and Shimon Edelman. 2008. Learn locally, act globally: Learning language from variation set cues. *Cognition*, 109(3):423–430.

Robert Östling. 2013. Stagger: an open-source part of speech tagger for swedish. *Northern European Journal of Language Technology*, 3:1–18.

Catherine E. Snow. 1972. Mothers' speech to children learning language. *Child Development*, 43(2):549–565.

Heidi R. Waterfall, Ben Sandbank, Luca Onnis, and Shimon Edelman. 2010. An empirical generative framework for computational modeling of language acquisition. *Journal of Child Language*, 37:671–703.

Heidi R. Waterfall. 2006. *A Little Change is a Good Thing: Feature Theory, Language Acquisition and Variation Sets.* Ph.D. thesis, Department of Linguistics, University of Chicago.

P. Wittenburg, H. Brugman, A. Russel, A. Klassmann, and H. Sloetjes. 2006. Elan: a professional framework for multimodality research. In *Proceedings of LREC 2006, Fifth International Conference on Language Resources and Evaluation*, pages 1556–1559, Genoa, Italy, May. ELRA.

Learning Phone Embeddings for Word Segmentation of Child-Directed Speech

Jianqiang Ma[a,b]   **Çağrı Çöltekin**[b]   **Erhard Hinrichs**[a,b]

[a] SFB 833, University of Tübingen, Germany

[b] Department of Linguistics, University of Tübingen, Germany

`{jma,ccoltekin,eh}@sfs.uni-tuebingen.de`

Abstract

This paper presents a novel model that learns and exploits embeddings of phone ngrams for word segmentation in child language acquisition. Embedding-based models are evaluated on a phonemically transcribed corpus of child-directed speech, in comparison with their symbolic counterparts using the common learning framework and features. Results show that learning embeddings significantly improves performance. We make use of extensive visualization to understand what the model has learned. We show that the learned embeddings are informative for both word segmentation and phonology in general.

1 Introduction

Segmentation is a prevalent problem in language processing. Both humans and computers process language as a combination of linguistic units, such as words. However, spoken language does not include reliable cues to word boundaries that are found in many writing systems. The hearers need to extract words from a continuous stream of sounds using their linguistic knowledge and the cues in the input signal. Although the problem is still non-trivial, competent language users utilize their knowledge of the input language, e.g., the (mental) lexicon, to a large extent to aid extraction of lexical units from the input stream.

Word segmentation in early language acquisition is especially interesting and challenging, as early language learners barely have a lexicon or any other linguistic knowledge to start with. Consequently, it has been studied extensively through psycholinguistic experiments (Cutler and Butterfield, 1992; Jusczyk et al., 1999; Jusczyk et al.,

1993; Saffran et al., 1996; Jusczyk et al., 1999; Suomi et al., 1997; van Kampen et al., 2008) and computational modeling (Cairns et al., 1994; Christiansen et al., 1998; Brent and Cartwright, 1996; Brent, 1999; Venkataraman, 2001; Xanthos, 2004; Goldwater et al., 2009; Johnson and Goldwater, 2009).

The majority of the state-of-the-art computational models use symbolic representations for input units. Due to Zipf's law, most linguistic units, however, are rare and thus the input provides little evidence for their properties that are useful for solving the task at hand. In machine learning terms, the learner has to deal with the data sparseness problem due to the rare units whose parameters cannot be estimated reliably. A model using distributed representations can counteract the data sparseness problem by exploiting the similarities between the units for parameter estimation. This has motivated the introduction of *embeddings* (Bengio et al., 2003; Collobert et al., 2011), a family of low-dimensional, real-valued vector representation of features that are learned from data. Unlike purely symbolic representations, such distributed representations allow input units that appear in similar contexts to share similar vectors (embeddings). The model can, then, exploit the similarities between the embeddings during segmentation and learning.

This paper studies the learning and use of embeddings of phone[1] uni- and bi-grams for computational models of word segmentation in child language acquisition. Our work is inspired by recent success of embeddings in NLP (Devlin et al., 2014; Socher et al., 2013), especially in Chinese word segmentation (Zheng et al., 2013; Pei et al., 2014; Ma and Hinrichs, 2015). However, this work differs from Chinese word segmenta-

---

[1] We use the therm *phone* as a theory-neutral term for the distinct (phonetic) segments in the input.

Proceedings of the 7th Workshop on Cognitive Aspects of Computational Language Learning, pages 53–63,
Berlin, Germany, August 11, 2016. ©2016 Association for Computational Linguistics

tion models in two aspects. (1) The model (Section 2) learns from a phonemically transcribed corpus of child-directed speech (Section 3.1) instead of large written text input. (2) The learning (Section 2.2) only relies on utterance boundaries in input as opposed to explicitly marked word boundaries. Although the number of phone types is small, higher level ngrams of phones inevitably increase the severity of data sparseness. Thus we expect embeddings to be particularly useful when larger phoneme ngrams are used as input units. The contributions of this paper are three-fold:

- A novel model that constructs and uses embeddings of phone ngrams for word segmentation in child language acquisition;

- Empirical evaluations of symbolic and embedding representations for this task on the benchmark data, which suggest that learning embeddings boosts the performance;

- A deeper analysis of the learned embeddings through visualizations and clustering, showing that the learned embeddings capture information relevant to segmentation and phonology in general.

In the next section we define the distributed representations we use in this study, *phone-embeddings*, and a method for learning the embeddings and the segmentation parameters simultaneously from a corpus without word boundaries. Then we present a set of experiments for comparing embedding and symbolic representations (Section 3). We show our visualization and clustering analyses of the learned embeddings (Section 4) before discussing our results further in the context of previous work (Section 5) and concluding the paper.

2 Learning Segmentation with Phone Embeddings

2.1 The architecture of the model

Figure 1 shows the architecture of the proposed embedding-based model. Our model takes the embeddings of phone uni- and bi-grams in the local window for each position in an utterance, and predicts whether that position is a word boundary. The embeddings for the phone ngrams are learned *jointly* with the segmentation model. The model has the following three components:

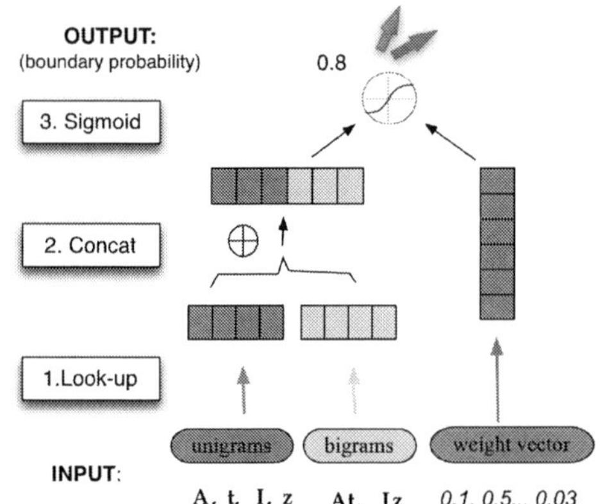

The position between t and I in "WAtIzIt" is being predicted.

Figure 1: Architecture of our model.

Look-up table maps phone ngrams to their corresponding embeddings. In this study, for each position j, we consider the 4 unigrams $(c_{j-1}, c_j, c_{j+1}, c_{j+2})$ and 2 bigrams ($c_{j-1}c_j$ and $c_{j+1}c_{j+2}$) that are in a window of 4 phones of positions j. The phone c_j represents the phone on the left of the current position j and so on.

Concatenation. To predict the segmentation for position j, the embeddings of the phone uni- and bi-gram features are *concatenated* into a single vector, *input embedding*, $\mathbf{i}_j \in \mathbb{R}^{NK}$, where $K = 6$ is the number of uni- and bi-gram used and $N = 50$ is the dimension of the embedding of each ngram.

Sigmoid function. The model then computes the sigmoid function (1) of the dot product of the input embedding $\mathbf{i}_j$ and the weight vector $\mathbf{w}$. The output is a score $\in [0, 1]$ that denotes the probability that the current position being a word boundary, which we call *boundary probability*.

$$f(j) = \frac{1}{1 + exp\left(-\mathbf{w} \cdot \mathbf{i}_j\right)} \tag{1}$$

2.2 Learning with utterance edge and random sampling

Our model learns from utterances that have word boundaries removed. It, however, utilizes the *utterance boundaries* as positive instances of word boundaries. Specifically, the position before the first phone of an utterance is the left boundary of the first word, and the position after the last phone of an utterance is the right boundary of the last word. For these positions, dummy symbols are used as the two leftmost (rightmost) phones. Moreover, one position within the utterance is randomly sampled as negative instance. Although such randomly sampled instances are not guaranteed to be actual negative ones, sampling balances the positive instances, which makes learning possible.

The training follows an on-line learning strategy, processing one utterance at a time and updating the parameters after processing each utterance. The trainable parameters are the weight vector and the embeddings of the uni- and bi-grams. For each position j, the boundary probability is computed with the current parameters. Then the parameters are updated by minimizing the *cross-entropy loss function* as in (2).

$$J_j = -\left[y_j \log f(j) + (1 - y_j) \log (1 - f(j)) \right] \quad (2)$$

In formula (2), $f(j)$ is the boundary probability estimated in (1) and y_j is its presumed value, which is 1 and 0 for utterance boundaries and sampled intra-utterance positions, respectively. To offset over-fitting, we add an L2 regularization term $(||\mathbf{i}_j||^2 + ||\mathbf{w}||^2)$ to the loss function, as follows:

$$J_j \leftarrow J_j + \frac{\lambda}{2} \left(||\mathbf{i}_j||^2 + ||\mathbf{w}||^2 \right) \quad (3)$$

The λ is a factor that adjusts the contribution of the regularization term. To minimize the regularized loss function, which is is still convex, we perform *stochastic gradient descent* to iteratively update the embeddings and the weight vector in turn, each time considering the other as constant. The gradients and update rules are similar to that of logistic regression model as in Tsuruoka et al. (2009), except that the input embeddings $\mathbf{i}$ are also updated besides the standard weight vector.

In particular, the gradient of input embeddings $\mathbf{i}_j$ for each particular position j is computed according to (4), where $\mathbf{w}$ is the weight vector and y_j is the assumed label. The input embeddings are then updated by (5), where α is the learning rate.

$$\frac{\partial J_j}{\partial \mathbf{i}_j} = (f(j) - y_j) \cdot \mathbf{w} + \lambda \mathbf{i}_j \quad (4)$$

$$\mathbf{i}_j \leftarrow \mathbf{i}_j - \alpha \frac{\partial J_j}{\partial \mathbf{i}_j} \quad (5)$$

2.3 Segmentation via greedy search

The word segmentation of utterances is a greedy search procedure using the learned model. It irreversibly predicts segmentation for each position j ($1 \le j \le N$ = utterance length), one at a time, in a left-to-right manner. If the boundary probability given by the model greater than 0.5, the current position is predicted as word boundary, otherwise non-boundary. The segmented word sequence is built from the predicted word boundaries in the utterance.

3 Experiments and Results

The learning framework described in Section 2 can also be adopted for symbolic representations where the ngram features for each position are represented by a sparse *binary vector*. In the symbolic representation, each distinct uni- or bi-gram is represented by a distinct dimension in the input vector. In that case, the learning framework is equivalent to a *logistic regression* model, the training of which only updates the weight vector but not the feature representations. In this section, we run experiments to compare the performances of embedding- and symbolic-based models using the same learning framework with the same features. Before presenting the experiments and the results, we describe the data and evaluation metrics.

3.1 Data

In the experiments reported in this paper, we use the *de facto* standard corpus for evaluating segmentation models. The corpus was collected by Bernstein Ratner (1987) and converted to a phonemic transcription by Brent and Cartwright (1996). The original corpus is part of the CHILDES database (MacWhinney and Snow, 1985). Following the convention in the literature, the corpus will be called the *BR corpus*. Since our model does not know the locations of true boundaries, we do not make training and test set distinction, following previous literature.

3.2 Evaluation metrics

As a measure of success, we report F-score, the harmonic mean of *precision* and *recall*. F-score is a well-known evaluation metric originated in information retrieval (van Rijsbergen, 1979). The calculation of these measures depend on true positive (TP), false positive (FP) and false negative (FN) values for each decision. Following earlier studies, we report three varieties of F-scores. The *boundary* F-score (**BF**) considers individual boundary decisions. The *word* F-score (**WF**) quantifies the accuracy of recognizing word tokens. And the *lexicon* F-scores (**LF**) are calculated based on the gold-standard lexicon and lexicon learned by the model. For details of the metrics, see Goldwater et al. (2009). Following the literature, the utterance boundaries are not included in boundary F-score calculations, while lexicon/word metrics include first and the last words in utterance.

Besides these standard scores we also present over-segmentation (**EO**) and under-segmentation (**EU**) error rate (lower is better) defined as:

$$ EO = \frac{FP}{FP + TN} \qquad EU = \frac{FN}{FN + TP} $$

where TN is true negatives of boundaries. Besides providing a different look at the models' behavior, it is straightforward to calculate the statistical uncertainty around them since they resemble N Bernoulli trials with a particular error rate, where N is number of boundary and word-internal positions for EU and EO respectively.

The results of our model in this paper are directly comparable with the results of previous work on the *BR corpus* using the above metrics. The utterance boundary information that our method uses is also available to any "pure" unsupervised method in literature, such as the EM-based algorithm of Brent (1999) and the Bayesian approach of Goldwater et al. (2009). In these methods, word hypotheses that cross utterance boundaries are not considered, which implicitly utilizes utterance boundary "supervision."

3.3 Experiments

To show the differences between the symbolic and embedding representations, we train both models on the *BR corpus*, and present the performance and error scores on the complete corpus. The training of all models use the linear decay scheme of learning rate with the initial value of 0.05 and the regularization factor is set to 0.001 throughout the experiments. Table 1 presents the results, including standard errors for EO and EU, for *emb*(edding)- and *sym*(bolic)-based models using unigram features (*uni*) and unigram+bigram features (*all*), respectively.

Table 1 shows the average of the results obtained from 10 independent runs. For each run, we take the scores from the 10th iteration of the whole data set, where the scores are stabilized. All models learn quickly and have good performance after

Model	EO	EU	BF	WF	LF
emb/all	**6.4**±**0.1**	**17.3**±**0.2**	**82.9**	**68.7**	**42.6**
sym/all	8.1±0.1	25.8±0.2	75.9	60.2	31.6
emb/uni	15.8±0.1	**10.6**±**0.3**	**77.4**	**59.1**	**40.7**
sym/uni	**13.2**±**0.1**	21.7±0.2	73.4	54.4	29.4

Table 1: Performance of embedding and symbolic models. Numbers in percentage.

the first iteration already. And the differences between the scores of subsequent iterations are rather small.

4 Visualization and Interpretation

The experiment results in the previous section show that learning embeddings jointly with a segmentation model, instead using symbolic representations, leads to a boost of segmentation performance. Nevertheless, it is not straightforward to interpret embeddings, as the "semantics" of each dimension is not pre-defined as in symbolic representations. In this section, we use visualization and clustering techniques to interpret the information captured by the embeddings.

Phone symbols in the BR corpus. We use the BR corpus for visualization as in the experiments. The transcription in the BR corpus use symbols that, unfortunately, can not be converted to International Phonetic Alphabet (IPA) in a context-free, deterministic way. Thus we keep them as they are and suggest readers who are unfamiliar with such symbols to refer to Appendix A.

4.1 Embeddings encode segmentation roles

Segmentation roles of phone ngrams. We first investigate the correspondence of the embeddings to the metrics that are indicative for segmentation decisions. For distinguishing word-boundary positions from word-internal positions as in segmentation models, it is helpful to know whether a particular phone unigram/bigram is more likely to occur at the beginning of a word (*word-initial*), at the end of a word (*word-final*), in the middle of a word (*word-medial*), or has a *balanced distribution* of above positions. For a phone bigram, it can also be *corss word-boundary*. We call such tendencies of phone ngrams as *segmentation roles*.

We hypothesize that the embeddings that are learned by our model can capture segmentation roles: the embeddings of phone ngrams of the same segmentation role are similar to each other and are dissimilar to the phone ngrams of different

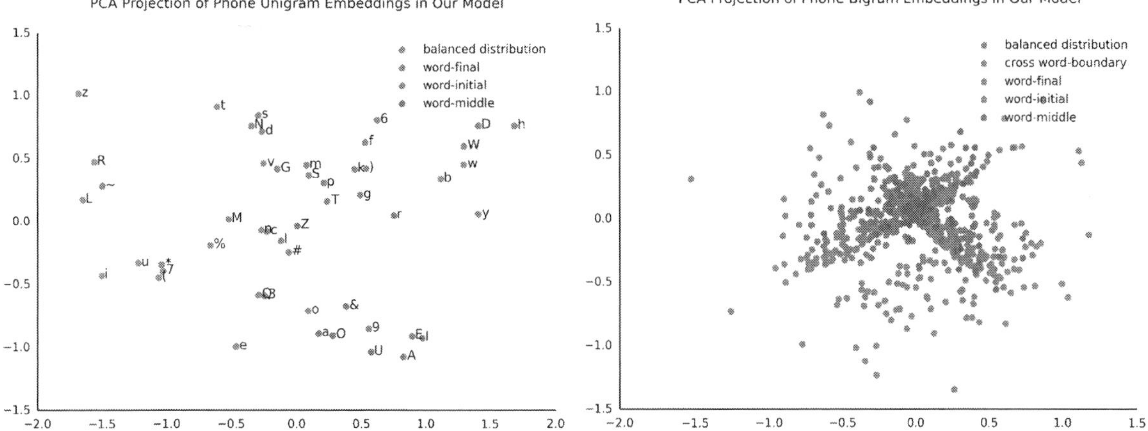

Figure 2: PCA Projections of the phone uni-gram (left) and bi-gram (right) embeddings learned in our model.

segmentation roles. To test this, we use principal component analysis (PCA) to project the embeddings of phone uni- and bi-grams that are learned in our model into two-dimension space, where the resulting vectors preserve 85% and 98% of the variance in the original 50-dimension uni- and bi-gram embeddings, respectively. We then plot such PCA-projected 2-D vectors of the phone ngrams in Figure 2, where the geometric distances between data points reflect the (dis-)similarities between the original embeddings of phone ngrams. These data points are color coded to demonstrate the dominant segmentation role of each phone ngram.

A phone ngram is categorized as *word-initial*, *word-medial*, *word-final* or *corss word-boundary* (only applicable for bigrams), if the ngram co-occur more than 50% of the time with the corresponding segmentation roles according to the gold standard segmentation. If none of the roles reaches the majority, the ngram is categorized as *balanced distribution*. Note that segmentation roles are assigned using the true word boundaries, while the embeddings are learned only from utterance boundaries.

Figure 2 (left) shows that phone unigrams of the same category tend to cluster in the same neighborhood, while unigrams of distinct categories tend to locate apart from each other. This is consistent with our hypothesis on embeddings being capable of capturing segmentation roles. Figure 2 (right) shows that the distribution of phone bigrams is noisier, as many bigrams of different cat-

egories congest in the center. This suggests that bigram embeddings are less well estimated than unigrams ones, probably due to the larger number and lower relative frequencies of bigrams. Nevertheless, the *word-initial* v.s. *word-final* contrast in bigrams is still sharp, as a result of our training procedure that makes heavy use of the initial and final positions of utterances, which are also word boundaries. In summary, the information that are encoded in our phone ngram embeddings is highly indicative of correct segmentations.

4.2 Embeddings capture phonology

Hierarchical clustering of phones. Different from the previous subsection that correlates the learned embeddings with segmentation-specific roles, we can alternatively explore the embeddings more freely to see what structures emerge from data. To this end, we apply *hierarchical agglomerative clustering* (Johnson, 1967) to the embeddings of phone unigrams to build up clusters in a bottom-up manner. Initially, each unigram embedding itself consists of a cluster. Then at each step, the two most similar clusters are merged. The procedure iterates until every embedding is in the same cluster. The similarity between clusters are computed by the single linkage method, which outputs the highest score of all the pairwise cosine similarities between the embeddings in the two clusters. Since the clustering procedure is based on pair-wise cosine similarities between embeddings, we first compute such similarity scores, composing the *similarity matrix*.

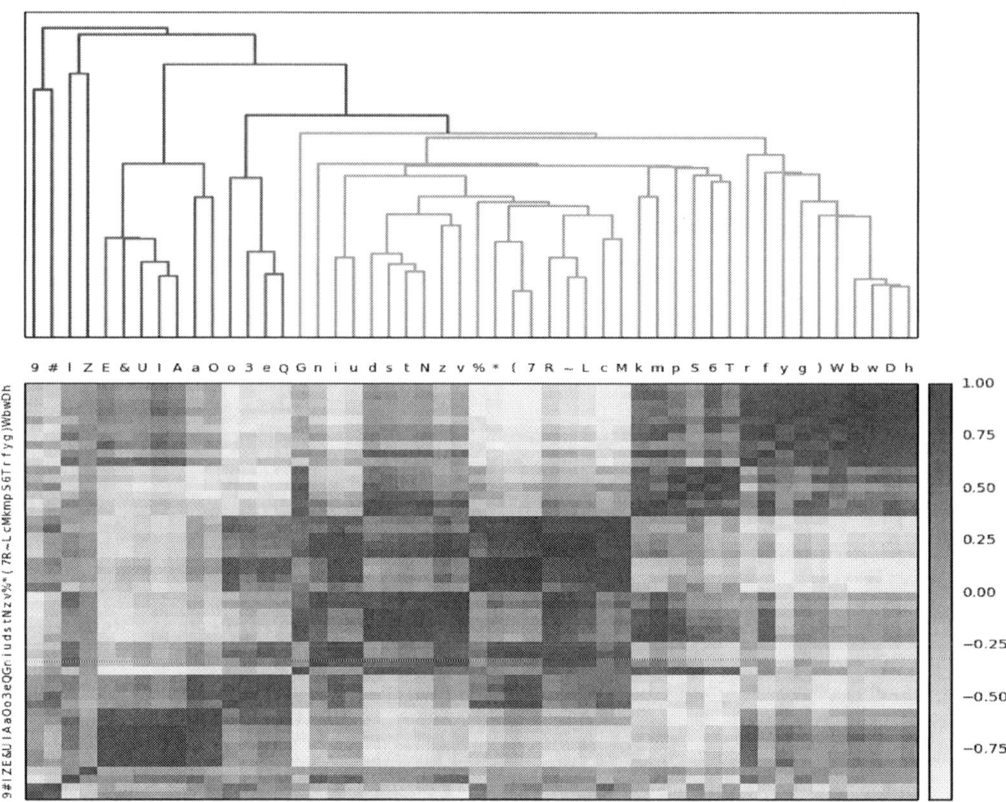

Figure 3: Hierarchical clustering and similarity matrix of phone embeddings learned by our model.

The *dendrogram* (Jones et al., 2001) that represents the clustering results is shown in Figure 3, together with the *heatmap* that represents the similarity matrix. The dendrogram draws a U-shaped link to indicate how a pair of child clusters form their parent cluster, where the dissimilarity between the two child clusters are shown by the height of the top of the U-link. The intensity of the color of each grid in the heatmap denotes the similarity between the two corresponding phone embeddings. Moreover, each lowest node, i.e. leaf, of the dendrogram is vertically aligned with the column of the heatmap that corresponds to the same phone, which is labeled using the BR-corpus symbols. Thus the dark blocks along the antidiagonal also indicate the salient clusters in which phone embeddings are similar to one another.

Phonological structure. The heatmap reveals several salient blocks, such as the one on the top-right corner and the one near the bottom-left corner. The former is part of a group of clusters spreading the whole right 2/3 of the dendrogram/heatmap, which mostly consists English

consonants. In contrast, the latter contains short, unrounded vowels in English, *E*, *&*, *I* and *A*, as in b*e*t, th*a*t, b*i*t and b*u*t, respectively. It also contains the long-short vowel pair *a* and *O* as in h*o*t and l*aw*. Immediately to the right of them are the cluster of compound vowels, *o*, *3*, *e*, *Q*. In general, most clusters are either consonant- or vowel-dominant, while groups of the similar vowels form sub-clusters under the big vowel cluster. Although far from perfect, the results suggest that the learned phone embeddings capture phonological features of English. On one hand, the emergence of such phonological structure is not surprising, as phonology is part of what defines a word, although our word segmentation model does not explicitly target it. On the other hand, such results are relevant as they suggest that the *phonological regularities are salient and learnable from transcriptions even if lexical knowledge is absent.*

4.3 Comparison with word2vec embeddings

We see that our phone embeddings can capture segmentation-informative and phonology-related

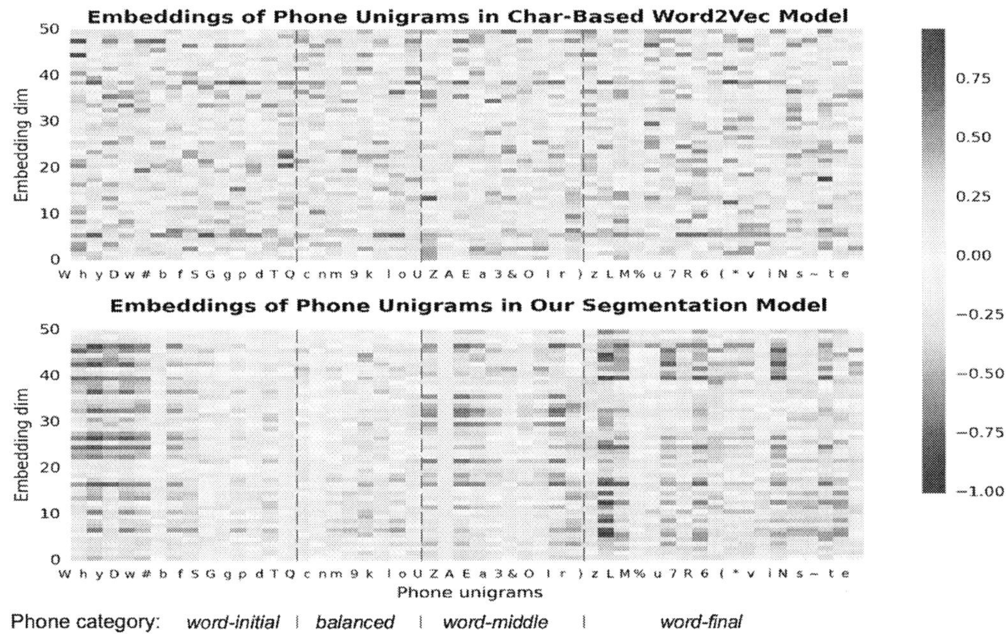

Figure 4: Heatmap of phone embeddings in word2vec (top) and our model (bottom).

patterns. A question remains: is this the consequence of joint learning of the embeddings with the segmentation model, or something also achievable by general-purpose embeddings? We test this by comparing our phone embeddings with the embeddings that are trained by a standard embedding construction tool, word2vec (Mikolov et al., 2013). We first preprocess the raw *BR corpus* to construct the phone uni- and bi-gram corpora, respectively. Then we run word2vec with *skip-gram* method for 20 iterations on the two corpora to train the embeddings for phone uni- and bi-grams, respectively. The training relies on using each ngram to predict other ngrams in the same local window. We use a window size of 4 phones in the training to be comparable with our models.

We first plot the heatmap of the unigram embeddings of the word2vec model and that of our model in Fig 4, where the embeddings of distinct phone categories in our model exhibit distinct patterns, whereas such distinctions are unclear in the word2vec embeddings. Then we conduct the same PCA and hierarchical clustering analyses for the word2vec embeddings, as we did for our learned embeddings. The results are shown in Figure 5 and 6, respectively. We see that word2vec embeddings capture neither segmentation-specific features nor phonological structures as our learned embeddings do, which suggests that the joint learning of the embeddings and the segmentation model is essential for the success.

5 Discussion and Related Work

Performance. The focus of this paper is investigating the usefulness of embeddings, rather than achieving best segmentation performance. Since multiple cues are useful for both segmentation by children (Mattys et al., 2005; Shukla et al., 2007) and computational models (Christiansen et al., 1998; Christiansen et al., 2005; Çöltekin and Nerbonne, 2014), our single-cue model is *not* expected to outperform multiple-cue ones. The upper part of Table 2 shows the results of two state-of-the-art systems, both of which adopt multiple cues. Goldwater et al. (2009) relies on Bayesian models, especially hierarchical Dirichlet process, which models phone unigrams, word unigrams and bigrams using similar distributions. Unlike our model, which has no explicit notion of words, Goldwater et al. (2009) keeps track of phones, words, as well as word bigrams. In comparison with our on-line learning approach, their Gibbs sampling-based learning method repeatedly processes the data in a batch way. By contrast, Çöltekin and Nerbonne (2014) does conduct on-line learning. But their best performing model,

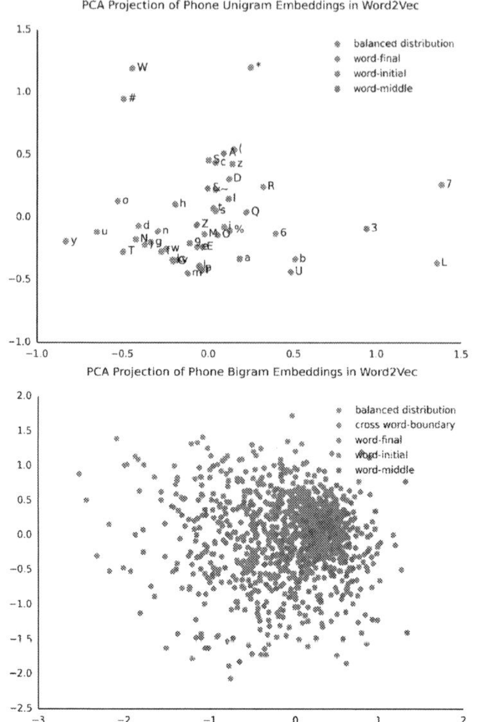

Figure 5: PCA Projections of the embeddings of phone unigrams (top) and bigrams (bottom) in word2vec models.

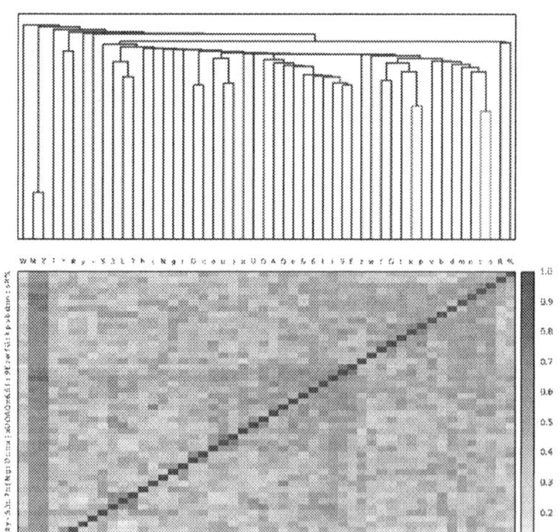

Figure 6: Hierarchical clustering and similarity matrix of phone embeddings in word2vec.

PUW, does not only rely on utterance boundaries (U) as in our model, but also combines the predictability information (P) and the lexicon (L) of previously discovered words.

An interesting observation is that our our model achieves reasonably good boundary and word-token F-scores, even comparing with these state-of-the-art models. Unfortunately, the lexicon F-score of our model is significantly lower. The reason is probably that our method models segmentation decisions per position without explicitly keeping a lexicon, whereas both state-of-the-art models are "lexicon-aware", which gives status to recognized words. The use of word context can help to identify low frequency words, some of which, especially longer ones, are difficult for our phone window-based model.

Model	BF	WF	LF
Goldwater et al. (2009)	85.2	72.3	**59.1**
Çöltekin and Nerbonne (2014): PUW	**87.3**	**76.4**	53.3
Daland and Pierrehumbert (2011)	62.7	42.5	10.1
Fleck (2008)	82.9	70.7	36.6
Çöltekin and Nerbonne (2014): U	83.8	71.1	44.9
Our model: embedding, uni- & bi-gram	82.9	68.7	42.6

Table 2: Comparisoin of the best performance of our model (bottom) with the state-of-the-art systems on the task (upper) and the models using utterance boundaries as the main cue (middle). U: using utterance boundary only; PUW: using predictability, utterance boundary and the learned lexicon. Numbers in percentage.

It is probably more instructive to compare the performance of our model with other models evaluated in similar settings and use utterance boundaries as the main cue. The results of such models are shown in the middle part of Table 2. Among them, Daland and Pierrehumbert (2011) uses only unigrams, whereas Fleck (2008) and the utterance boundary-based model (U) in Çöltekin and Nerbonne (2014) are more elaborate, combining one to three-grams of phones. The performance would probably be lower if only uni- or bigrams are used as in our model.

The scores at the bottom of the Table 2 suggest that our model fares well in comparison to the models that exploit similar learning strategies and information sources. The results also show that embeddings of phone unigrams and bigrams are effective for segmentation. In addition, we also tried trigrams, which did not improve the results for symbolic or embedding models. This may be due to that the trigrams are too sparse, especially when our training samples only one inter-utterance position per utterance.

Model properties and design choice. As described at the beginning of Section 3, the proposed model can be seen as an extension to logistic regression model, where the resulting model also learns the distributed representations of features from the data. The training relies on isolated positions, namely utterance boundaries and sampled intra-utterance positions, making the model a classifier that ignores the sequential dependencies. For these reasons, our model is structurally simple and computationally efficient. We also avoid batch processing-based and computationally expensive techniques such as Gibbs sampling, as adopted in many Bayesian models. For cognitive modeling, efficient, on-line learning is favorable, as human brain appears to work that way.

To investigate the impact of learning and using distributed representations, we could alternatively use other neural network architectures, such as multi-layer feed-forward neural networks or recurrent neural networks. The computational complexity would be much higher in that case. Nevertheless, it is still interesting, as a future work, to develop phone-level recurrent neural network (RNN) models for the task. In particular, it may be promising to experiment with a modern variation of RNN, long short-term memory (Schmidhuber and Hochreiter, 1997), as it recently achieved considerable success on various NLP tasks. A challenge here is how to train effective RNN models in the language acquisition setting, where explicit supervision is mostly absent.

Embeddings boost segmentation. Table 1 demonstrates that learning embeddings instead of using symbolic representations boosts segmentation performance. This is true in both settings where the model adopts unigrams and unigram+bigrams as features, respectively. With embeddings, models apply the information obtained from frequent input units to the decisions involving infrequent units with similar representations. Hence, although embeddings are beneficial in both settings, it is not surprising that the improvement is higher for the unigrams+bigrams setting, where the data sparseness is more severe.

Figure 7 shows the difference in the learning curves of the embedding-based and symbolic-based models, both using unigram+bigram features. The embedding model starts with a higher error rate in comparison to the symbolic one, since the vectors for each unit is randomly initialized. However, as the embeddings are updated with more input, the embedding model quickly catches

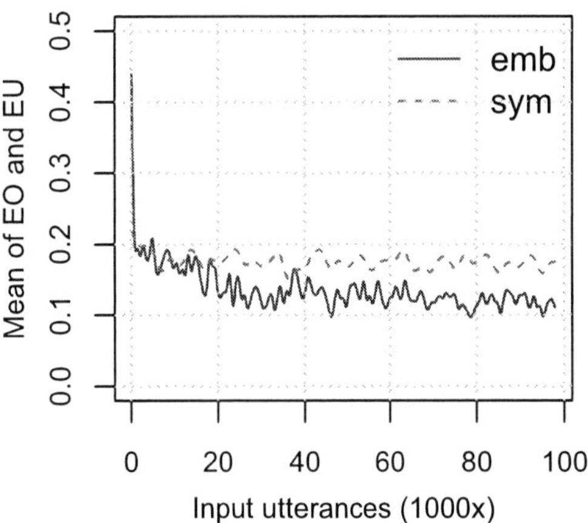

Figure 7: The mean of the error rates during the 1st iteration for the *emb*edding and *sym*bolic models.

up with the symbolic model and finally outperforms it, as the results in Table 1 show.

Other distributed representations. The utterance boundary cue has been used in earlier work (Aslin et al., 1996; Stoianov and Nerbonne, 2000; Xanthos, 2004; Monaghan and Christiansen, 2010; Fleck, 2008), but not with embeddings. Distributed representations other than learned embeddings, however, have been common in the early connectionist models (Cairns et al., 1994; Aslin et al., 1996; Christiansen et al., 1998). Besides better performance, our model differs in that it learns the embeddings from the input, while earlier models used hand-crafted distributed representations. This allows our model to optimize representations for the task at hand.

6   Conclusion

In this paper, we have presented a model that jointly learns word segmentation and the embeddings of phone ngrams. The learning in our model is guided by the utterance boundaries. Hence, our learning method, although not unsupervised in machine learning terms, does not use any information that is unavailable to the children acquiring language. To the best of our knowledge, this is the first work of learning phone embeddings for computational models of word segmentation in child language acquisition. Compared with symbolic-based models using the same learning framework, embedding-based models significantly improve results. Visualization and analyses show that the learned embeddings are indicative of not only correct segmentations, but also certain phonological structures.

Acknowledgments

The authors would like to thank the anonymous reviewers for their helpful comments and suggestions. The financial support for the research reported in this paper was partly provided by the German Research Foundation (DFG) via the Collaborative Research Center "The Construction of Meaning" (SFB 833), project A3.

References

Richard N. Aslin, Julide Z. Woodward, Nicholas P. LaMendola, and Thomas G. Bever. 1996. Models of word segmentation in fluent maternal speech to infants. In James L. Morgan and Katherine Demuth, editors, *Signal to Syntax: Bootstrapping From Speech to Grammar in Early Acquisition*, chapter 8, pages 117–134. Lawrence Erlbaum Associates.

Yoshua Bengio, Réjean Ducharme, Pascal Vincent, and Christian Janvin. 2003. A neural probabilistic language model. *The Journal of Machine Learning Research*, 3:1137–1155.

Nan Bernstein Ratner. 1987. The phonology of parent-child speech. In K. Nelson and A. van Kleeck, editors, *Children's language*, volume 6, pages 159–174. Erlbaum, Hillsdale, NJ.

Michael R. Brent and Timothy A. Cartwright. 1996. Distributional regularity and phonotactic constraints are useful for segmentation. *Cognition*, 61:93–125.

Michael R. Brent. 1999. An efficient, probabilistically sound algorithm for segmentation and word discovery. *Machine Learning*, 34(1-3):71–105.

Paul Cairns, Richard Shillcock, Nick Chater, and Joe Levy. 1994. Modelling the acquisition of lexical segmentation. In *Proceedings of the 26th Child Language Research Forum*. University of Chicago Press.

Çağrı Çöltekin and John Nerbonne. 2014. An explicit statistical model of learning lexical segmentation using multiple cues. In *Proceedings of EACL 2014 Workshop on Cognitive Aspects of Computational Language Learning*.

Çağrı Çöltekin. 2011. *Catching Words in a Stream of Speech: Computational simulations of segmenting transcribed child-directed speech*. Ph.D. thesis, University of Groningen.

Morten H. Christiansen, Joseph Allen, and Mark S. Seidenberg. 1998. Learning to segment speech using multiple cues: A connectionist model. *Language and Cognitive Processes*, 13(2):221–268.

Morten H. Christiansen, Christopher M. Conway, and Suzanne Curtin. 2005. Multiple-cue integration in language acquisition: A connectionist model of speech segmentation and rule-like behavior. In J.W. Minett and W.S.-Y. Wang, editors, *Language acquisition, change and emergence: Essays in evolutionary linguistics*, chapter 5, pages 205–249. City University of Hong Kong Press, Hong Kong.

Ronan Collobert, Jason Weston, Léon Bottou, Michael Karlen, Koray Kavukcuoglu, and Pavel Kuksa. 2011. Natural language processing (almost) from scratch. *The Journal of Machine Learning Research*, 12:2493–2537.

Anne Cutler and Sally Butterfield. 1992. Rhythmic cues to speech segmentation: Evidence from juncture misperception. *Journal of Memory and Language*, 31(2):218–236.

Robert Daland and Janet B Pierrehumbert. 2011. Learning diphone-based segmentation. *Cognitive Science*, 35(1):119–155.

Jacob Devlin, Rabih Zbib, Zhongqiang Huang, Thomas Lamar, Richard Schwartz, and John Makhoul. 2014. Fast and robust neural network joint models for statistical machine translation. In *Proceedings of ACL*, pages 1370–1380.

Margaret M. Fleck. 2008. Lexicalized phonotactic word segmentation. In *Proceedings of the Annual Meeting of the Association of Computational Linguistics (ACL-08)*, pages 130–138.

Sharon Goldwater, Thomas L. Griffiths, and Mark Johnson. 2009. A Bayesian framework for word segmentation: Exploring the effects of context. *Cognition*, 112:21–54.

Mark Johnson and Sharon Goldwater. 2009. Improving nonparameteric Bayesian inference: experiments on unsupervised word segmentation with adaptor grammars. In *Proceedings of Human Language Technologies: The 2009 Annual Conference of the North American Chapter of the Association for Computational Linguistics*, pages 317–325.

Stephen C Johnson. 1967. Hierarchical clustering schemes. *Psychometrika*, 32(3):241–254.

Eric Jones, Travis Oliphant, Pearu Peterson, et al. 2001–. SciPy: Open source scientific tools for Python. [Online; accessed 2016-04-29].

Peter W. Jusczyk, Anne Cutler, and Nancy J. Redanz. 1993. Infants' preference for the predominant stress patterns of English words. *Child Development*, 64(3):675–687.

Peter W. Jusczyk, Derek M. Houston, and Mary Newsome. 1999. The beginnings of word segmentation in English-learning infants. *Cognitive Psychology*, 39:159–207.

Jianqiang Ma and Erhard Hinrichs. 2015. Accurate linear-time Chinese word segmentation via embedding matching. In *Proceedings of ACL-IJCNLP (Volume 1: Long Papers)*, pages 1733–1743, Beijing, China, July. Association for Computational Linguistics.

Brian MacWhinney and Catherine Snow. 1985. The child language data exchange system. *Journal of Child Language*, 12(2):271–269.

Sven L. Mattys, Laurence White, and James F. Melhorn. 2005. Integration of multiple speech segmentation cues: A hierarchical framework. *Journal of Experimental Psychology: General*, 134(4):477–500.

Tomas Mikolov, Ilya Sutskever, Kai Chen, Greg S Corrado, and Jeff Dean. 2013. Distributed representations of words and phrases and their compositionality. In *Advances in neural information processing systems*, pages 3111–3119.

Padraic Monaghan and Morten H. Christiansen. 2010. Words in puddles of sound: modelling psycholinguistic effects in speech segmentation. *Journal of Child Language*, 37(Special Issue 03):545–564.

Wenzhe Pei, Tao Ge, and Chang Baobao. 2014. Max-margin tensor neural network for chinese word segmentation. In *Proceedings of ACL*, pages 239–303.

Jenny R. Saffran, Richard N. Aslin, and Elissa L. Newport. 1996. Statistical learning by 8-month old infants. *Science*, 274(5294):1926–1928.

Jürgen Schmidhuber and Sepp Hochreiter. 1997. Long short-term memory. *Neural computation*, 7(8):1735–1780.

Mohinish Shukla, Marina Nespor, and Jacques Mehler. 2007. An interaction between prosody and statistics in the segmentation of fluent speech. *Cognitive Psychology*, 54(1):1–32.

Richard Socher, John Bauer, Christopher D Manning, and Andrew Y Ng. 2013. Parsing with compositional vector grammars. In *Proceedings of ACL*, pages 455–465.

Ivelin Stoianov and John Nerbonne. 2000. Exploring phonotactics with simple recurrent networks. In Frank van Eynde, Ineke Schuurman, and Ness Schelkens, editors, *Proceedings of Computational Linguistics in the Netherlands 1999*, pages 51–67.

Kari Suomi, James M. McQueen, and Anne Cutler. 1997. Vowel harmony and speech segmentation in finnish. *Journal of Memory and Language*, 36(3):422–444.

Yoshimasa Tsuruoka, Jun'ichi Tsujii, and Sophia Ananiadou. 2009. Stochastic gradient descent training for L1-regularized log-linear models with cumulative penalty. In *Proceedings of ACL-IJCNLP*, pages 477–485.

Anja van Kampen, Güliz Parmaksız, Ruben van de Vijver, and Barbara Höhle. 2008. Metrical and statistical cues for word segmentation: The use of vowel harmony and word stress as cues to word boundaries by 6- and 9month-old Turkish learners. In Anna Gavarro and M. Joao Freitas, editors, *Language Acquisition and Development: Proceedings of GALA 2007*, pages 313–324.

C. J. van Rijsbergen. 1979. *Information Retrieval*. Butterworth-Heinemann, 2nd edition.

Anand Venkataraman. 2001. A statistical model for word discovery in transcribed speech. *Computational Linguistics*, 27(3):351–372.

Aris Xanthos. 2004. An incremental implementation of the utterance-boundary approach to speech segmentation. In *Proceedings of Computational Linguistics in the Netherlands (CLIN) 2003*, pages 171–180.

Xiaoqing Zheng, Hanyang Chen, and Tianyu Xu. 2013. Deep learning for Chinese word segmentation and pos tagging. In *Proceedings of EMNLP*, pages 647–657.

A Symbols used in BR corpus

Consonants		Vowels		Rhotic Vowels	
Symbol	Example	Symbol	Example	Symbol	Example
D	the	&	that	#	are
G	jump	6	about	%	for
L	bottle	7	bOy	(	here
M	rhythm	9	fly	)	lure
N	sing	A	but	*	hair
S	ship	E	bet	3	bird
T	thin	I	bit	R	butter
W	when	O	law		
Z	azure	Q	bout		
b	boy	U	put		
c	chip	a	hot		
d	dog	e	bay		
f	fox	i	bee		
g	go	o	boat		
h	hat	u	boot		
k	cut				
l	lamp				
m	man				
n	net				
p	pipe				
r	run				
s	sit				
t	toy				
v	view				
w	we				
y	you				
z	zip				
~	button				

Adapted from Çöltekin (2011).

Generalization in Artificial Language Learning:
Modelling the Propensity to Generalize

Raquel G. Alhama, Willem Zuidema
Institute for Logic, Language and Computation
University of Amsterdam, The Netherlands
{rgalhama, w.h.zuidema}@uva.nl

Abstract

Experiments in Artificial Language Learning have revealed much about the cognitive mechanisms underlying sequence and language learning in human adults, in infants and in non-human animals. This paper focuses on their ability to generalize to novel grammatical instances (i.e., instances consistent with a familiarization pattern). Notably, the propensity to generalize appears to be negatively correlated with the amount of exposure to the artificial language, a fact that has been claimed to be contrary to the predictions of statistical models (Peña et al. (2002); Endress and Bonatti (2007)). In this paper, we propose to model generalization as a three-step process, and we demonstrate that the use of statistical models for the first two steps, contrary to widespread intuitions in the ALL-field, can explain the observed decrease of the propensity to generalize with exposure time.

1 Introduction

In the last twenty years, experiments in Artificial Language Learning (ALL) have become increasingly popular for the study of the basic mechanisms that operate when subjects are exposed to language-like stimuli. Thanks to these experiments, we know that 8 month old infants can segment a speech stream by extracting statistical information of the input, such as the transitional probabilities between adjacent syllables (Saffran et al. (1996a); Aslin et al. (1998)). This ability also seems to be present in human adults (Saffran et al., 1996b), and to some extent in nonhuman animals like cotton-top tamarins (Hauser et al., 2001) and rats (Toro and Trobalón, 2005).

Even though this statistical mechanism is well attested for segmentation, it has been claimed that it does not suffice for generalization to novel stimuli or *rule learning*[1]. Ignited by a study by Marcus et al. (1999), which postulated the existence of an additional *rule-based* mechanism for generalization, a vigorous debate emerged around the question of whether the evidence from ALL-experiments supports the existence of a specialized mechanism for generalization (Peña et al. (2002); Onnis et al. (2005); Endress&Bonatti (2007); Frost&Monaghan (2016); Endress&Bonatti (2016)), echoing earlier debates about the supposed dichotomy between rules and statistics (Chomsky, 1957; Rumelhart and McClelland, 1986; Pinker and Prince, 1988; Pereira, 2000).

From a Natural Language Processing perspective, the dichotomy between rules and statistics is unhelpful. In this paper, we therefore propose a different conceptualization of the steps involved in generalization in ALL. In the following sections, we will first review some of the experimental data that has been interpreted as evidence for an additional generalization mechanism (Peña et al. (2002); Endress&Bonatti (2007); Frost&Monaghan (2016)). We then reframe the interpretation of those results with our 3-step approach, a proposal of the main steps that are required for generalization, involving: (i) memorization of segments of the input, (ii) computation of the probability for unseen sequences, and (iii) distribution of this probability among particular unseen sequences. We model the first step with the *Retention&Recognition* model (Alhama et al., 2016). We propose that a rational charac-

---

[1] We prefer the term 'generalization' because 'rule-learning' can be confused with a particular theory of generalization that claims that the mental structures used in the generalization process have the form of algebraic rules.

Proceedings of the 7th Workshop on Cognitive Aspects of Computational Language Learning, pages 64–72,
Berlin, Germany, August 11, 2016. ©2016 Association for Computational Linguistics

terization of the second step can be accomplished with the use of *smoothing* techniques (which we further demonstrate with the use of the Simple Good-Turing method, (Good&Turing (1953); Gale (1995)). We then argue that the modelling results shown in these two steps already account for the key aspects of the experimental data; and importantly, it removes the need to postulate an additional, separate generalization mechanism.

2 Experimental Record

Peña et al. (2002) conduct a series of Artificial Language Learning experiments in which French-speaking adults are familiarized to a synthesized speech stream consisting of a sequence of artificial *words*. Each of these words contains three syllables A_iXC_i such that the A_i syllable always co-occurs with the C_i syllable (as indicated by the subindex i). This forms a consistent pattern (a "rule") consisting in a non-adjacent dependency between A_i and C_i, with a middle syllable X that varies. The order of the words in the stream is randomized, with the constraint that words do not appear consecutively if they either: (i) belong to the same "family" (i.e., they have the same A_i and C_i syllables), or (ii) they have the same middle syllable X.

stream	pulikiberagatafodupuraki..
words A_iXC_i	puliki, beraga, tafodu, ...
part-words C_jA_iX, XC_iA_j	kibera, ragata, gatafo, ...
rule-words A_iYC_i	pubeki, beduga, takidu, ...
class-words A_iYC_j	pubedu, betaki, tapuga, ...
rule*-words A_iZC_i	puveki, bezoga, tathidu, ...

Table 1: Summary of the stimuli used in the depicted experiments.

After the familiarization phase, the participants respond a two-alternative forced choice test. The two-alternatives involve a word vs. a *part-word*, or a word vs. a *rule-word*, and the participants are asked to judge which item seemed to them more like a word of the imaginary language they had listened to. A part-word is an ill-segmented sequence of the form XC_iA_j or C_iA_jX; a choice for a part-word over a word is assumed to indicate that the word was not correctly extracted from the stream. A rule-word is a rule-obeying sequence that involves a "novel" middle syllable Y (mean-

ing that Y did not appear in the stream as an X, although it did appear as an A or C). Rule-words are therefore a particular generalization from words. Table 1 shows examples of these type of test items.

In their baseline experiment, the authors expose the participants to a 10 minute stream of A_iXC_i words. In the subsequent test phase, the subjects show a significant preference for words over part-words, proving that the words could be segmented out of the familiarization stream. In a second experiment the same setup is used, with the exception that the test now involves a choice between a part-word and a rule-word. The subjects' responses in this experiment do not show a significant preference for either part-words or rule-words, suggesting that participants do not generalize to novel grammatical sequences. However, when the authors, in a third experiment, insert micropauses of 25ms between the words, the participants do show a preference for rule-words over part-words. A shorter familiarization (2 minutes) containing micropauses also results in a preference for rule-words; in contrast, a longer familiarization (30 minutes) without the micropauses results in a preference for part-words. In short, the presence of micropauses seems to facilitate generalization to rule-words, while the amount of exposure time correlates negatively with this capacity.

Endress and Bonatti (2007) report a range of experiments with the same familiarization procedure used by Peña et al. However, their test for generalization is based on *class-words*: unseen sequences that start with a syllable of class "A" and end with a syllable of class "C", but with A and C not appearing in the same triplet in the familiarization (and therefore not forming a nonadjacent dependency).

From the extensive list of experiments conducted by the authors, we will refer only to those that test the preference between words and class-words, for different amounts of exposure time. The results for those experiments (illustrated in figure 1) also show that the preference for generalized sequences decreases with exposure time. For short exposures (2 and 10 minutes) there is a significant preference for class-words; when the exposure time is increased to 30 minutes, there is no preference for either type of sequence, and in a 60 minutes exposure, the preference reverses to part-words.

Finally, Frost and Monaghan (2016) show that

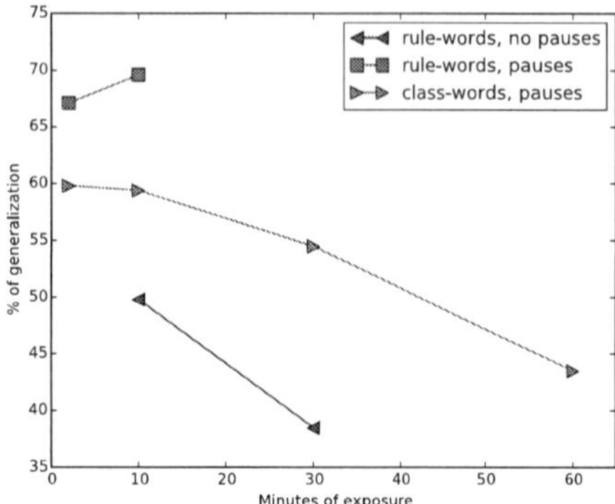

Figure 1: Percentage of choices for rule-words and class-words, in the experiments reported in Peña et al. (2002) and Endress&Bonatti (2007), for different exposure times to the familiarization stream.

micropauses are not essential for rule-like generalization to occur. Rather, the degree of generalization depends on the type of test sequences. The authors notice that the middle syllables used in rule-words might actually discourage generalization, since those syllables appear in a different position in the stream. Therefore, they test their participants with *rule*-words*: sequences of the form $A_i Z C_i$, where A_i and C_i co-occur in the stream, and Z does not appear. After a 10 minute exposure without pauses, participants show a clear preference for the rule*-words over part-words of the form $Z C_i A_j$ or $C_i A_j Z$.

The pattern of results is complex, but we can identify the following key findings: (i) generalization for a stream without pauses is only manifested for rule*-words, but not for rule-words nor class-words; (ii) the preference for rule-words and class-words is boosted if micropauses are present; (iii) increasing the amount of exposure time correlates negatively with generalization to rule-words and class-words (with differences depending on the type of generalization and the presence of micropauses, as can be seen in figure 1). This last phenomenon, which we call *time effect*, is precisely the aspect we want to explain with our model. (Note, in figure 1, that in the case of rule-words and pauses, the amount of generalization increases a tiny bit with exposure time, contrary to the time effect. We cannot test whether this is a significant difference, since we do not have access to the data. Endress&Bonatti, however, provided convincing statistical analysis supporting a signif-

icant inverse correlation between exposure time and generalization to class-words).

3 Understanding the generalization mechanism: a 3-step approach

Peña et al. interpret their findings as support for the theory that there are at least two mechanisms, which get activated in the human brain based on different cues in the input. Endress and Bonatti adopt that conclusion (and name it the *More-than-One-Mechanism* hypothesis, or *MoM*), and moreover claim that this additional mechanism cannot be based on statistical computations. The authors predict that statistical learning would benefit from increasing the amount of exposure:

> *"If participants compute the generalizations by a single associationist mechanism, then they should benefit from an increase in exposure, because longer experience should strengthen the representations built by associative learning (whatever these representations may be)."* (Endress and Bonatti, 2007)

We think this argument is based on a wrong premise: stronger representations do not necessarily entail greater generalization. On the contrary, we argue that even very basic models of statistical smoothing make the opposite prediction. To demonstrate this in a model that can be compared to empirical data, we propose to think about the process of generalization in ALL as involving the following steps (illustrated also in figure 2):

(i) **Memorization:** Build up a memory store of segments with frequency information (i.e., compute subjective frequencies).

(ii) **Quantification of the propensity to generalize:** Depending on the frequency information from (i), decide how likely are other unseen types.

(iii) **Distribution of probability over possible generalizations:** Distribute the probability for unseen types computed in (ii), assigning a probability to each generalized sequence.

Crucially, we believe that step (ii) has been neglected in ALL models of generalization. This step accounts for the fact that generalization is

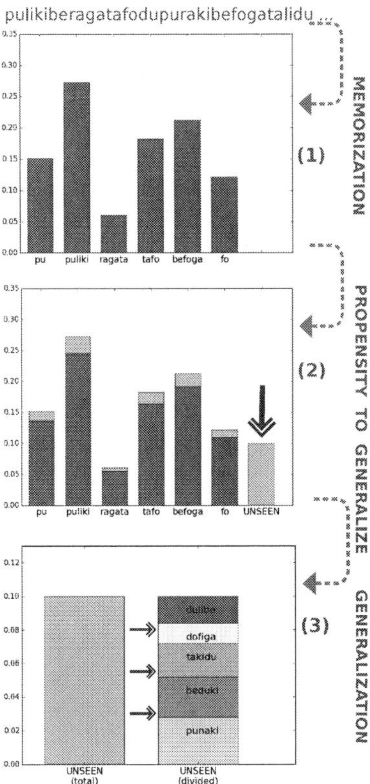

Figure 2: Three step approach to generalization: (1) memorization of segments, (2) compute probability of new items, and (3) distribute probability between possible new items.

not only based on the particular structure underlying the stimuli, but also depends on the statistical properties of the input.

At this point, we can already reassess the MoM hypothesis: more exposure time does entail better representation of the stimuli (as would be reflected in step (i)), but the impact of exposure time on generalization depends on the model used for step (ii). Next, we show that a cognitive model of step (i) and a rational statistical model of step (ii) already account for the *time effect*.

4 Memorization of segments: the *Retention and Recognition* model

For step (i) of our approach, several existing models maybe used, including models based on recurrent neural networks (Seidenberg and Elman, 1999), autoencoders (French et al., 2011; French and Cottrell, 2014), exemplar-based pro-

cessing (Perruchet and Vinter, 1998) and nonparametric Bayesian inference (Goldwater et al., 2006). We have decided to implement the Retention&Recognition (R&R) model, proposed in (Alhama et al., 2016). R&R is a probabilistic exemplar-based model that has been shown to fit experimental data from a range of ALL experiments on segmentation, and, importantly, produces very skewed frequency distributions that fit well with our intuition about step (ii).

Starting from an initially empty memory, R&R processes subsequences (segments) of the speech stream, and decides probabilistically whether those segments will be stored in its internal memory. The output of the model is a memory of segments, each one with a count of how many times the model has decided to store it in memory. The authors refer to these counts as *subjective frequencies*.

In each iteration, R&R is presented with one segment from the input stream. Each segment may be composed of any number of syllables (until an arbitrarily set maximum). For instance, for a stream starting with *talidupuraki...*, the model would be presented, in order, with the segments *ta, tali, talidu, talidupu, li, lidu, lidupu, lidupura*, etc. (assuming a maximum length of four syllables).

Each one of these segments is processed as shown in figure 3: first, the recognition mechanism attempts to recognize the segment (that is, it attempts to determine whether the segment corresponds to one of the segments already in memory). If the attempt succeeds, the subjective frequency (*count*) of the segment in memory is increased with one. If the segment was not recognized, the model may still retain it. If it does, the segment will be added to the memory (or, if already there from a previous iteration, its subjective frequency is increased with one). If not, the segment is ignored, and the next segment is processed.

The recognition probability p_1 for segment s is defined as follows (eq. 1):

$$p_1(s) = \left(1 - B^{activation(s)}\right) \cdot D^{\#types} \quad (1)$$

$$0 \leqslant B, D \leqslant 1$$

where B and D are parameters to be set with the empirical data. The recognition probability depends on the *activation* of the segment, which equals the subjective frequency. As it can be deduced from eq. 1, segments with greater subjec-

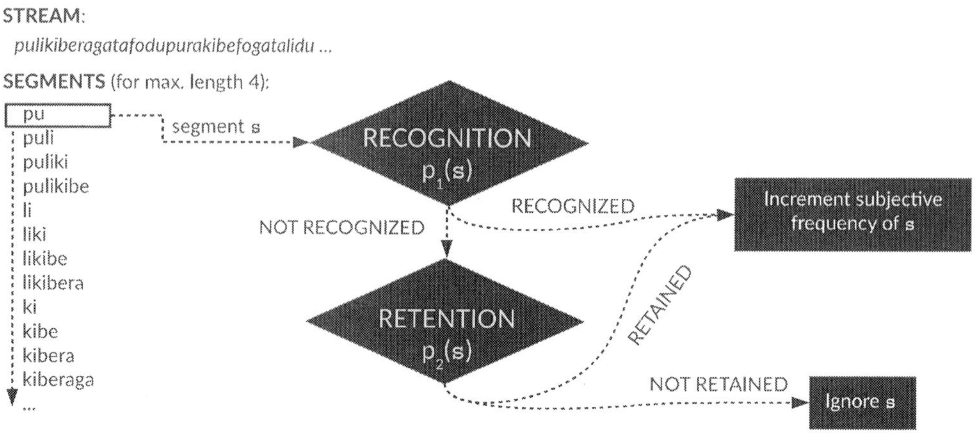

Figure 3: The Retention&Recognition model. Diagram based on Alhama et al. (2016).

tive frequency are easier to recognize. However, the number of different segment types in memory ($\#types$) makes the recognition task more difficult.

The retention probability p_2 is defined in eq. 2:

$$p_2(s) = A^{length(s)} \cdot C^{\pi} \qquad (2)$$

$$0 \leqslant A, C \leqslant 1; \quad \pi = \begin{cases} 0 \text{ after a pause} \\ 1 \text{ otherwise} \end{cases}$$

A and C are parameters to be set with empirical data, and π takes the value 0 when the segment being processed occurs right after a pause, and 1 otherwise. The retention probability is greater for shorter segments (as can be deduced from the $length(s)$ exponent applied to an A parameter that ranges between 0 and 1). The C parameter, which is again between 0 and 1, attenuates this probability unless a pause precedes the segment. This has the effect of boosting the retention of segments that appear after a pause.

The four parameters involved in the model (A, B, C, D) set the contribution of each of its components, and allow for the adaptation of the model to different tasks or species. Alhama et al. did not report the optimal parameter setting for the experiments we are concerned with here, but they assert that the main qualitative features of the model (such as the *rich-get-richer* dynamics of the recognition function) are independent of the parameters.

Among these qualitative features, one that is particularly relevant for our study is the *skew* that can be observed in the subjective frequencies computed by the model. This feature, which can be observed in figure 4, is presented in the original paper as being in consonance with empirical data. Here, we show that this property can also be validated in a different way: when R&R is part of a pipeline of models (like the 3-step approach), the skew turns out to be a necessary property for the success of the next model in the sequence. We come back to this point in section 7.

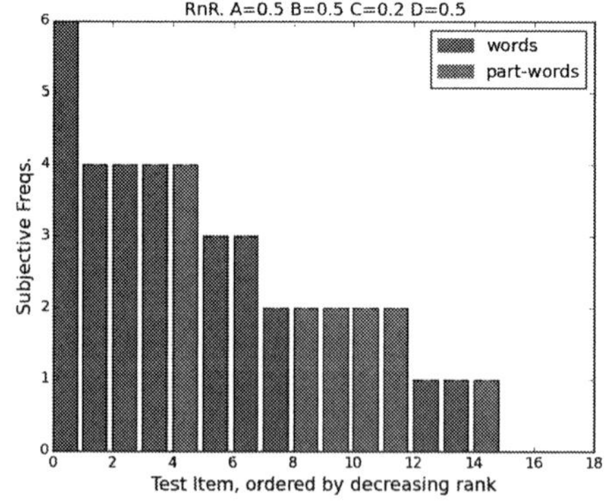

Figure 4: Subjective frequencies computed by the R&R model (A=0.5, B=0.5, C=0.2, D=0.5), for an exposure of 10 minutes (without pauses) to the stimuli used by Peña et al.

5 Quantifying the propensity to generalize: the Simple Good-Turing method

In probabilistic modelling, generalization must necessarily involve shifting probability mass from attested events to unattested events. This is a well known problem in Natural Language Processing, and the techniques to deal with it are known as *smoothing*. Here, we explore the use of the Simple Good Turing (Gale and Sampson, 1995) smoothing method as a computational level characterization of the propensity to generalize.

Simple Good-Turing (SGT), a computationally efficient implementation of the Good-Turing method (Good, 1953), is a technique to estimate the frequency of unseen types, based on the frequency of already observed types. The method works as follows: we take the subjective frequencies r computed by R&R and, for each of them, we compute the frequency of that frequency (N_r), that is, the number of sequences that have a certain subjective frequency r. The values N_r are then *smoothed*, that is re-estimated with a continuous downward-sloping line in log space. The smoothed values $S(N_r)$ are used to reestimate the frequencies according to (3):

$$r^* = (r+1)\frac{S(N_{r+1})}{S(N_r)} \qquad (3)$$

The probabilities for frequency classes are then computed based on these reestimated frequencies:

$$p_r = \frac{r^*}{N} \qquad (4)$$

where N is the total of the unnormalized estimates[2].

Finally, the probability for unseen events is computed based on the (estimated)[3] probability of types of frequency one, with the following equation:

$$P_0 = \frac{S(N_1)}{N} \qquad (5)$$

This probability P_0 corresponds to what we have called "propensity to generalize".

As can be deduced from the equations, SGT is designed to ensure that the probability for unseen types is similar to the probability of types with frequency one. The propensity to generalize is therefore greater for distributions where most of the probability mass is for smaller frequencies. This obeys a rational principle: when types have been observed with high frequency, it is likely that all the types in the population have already been attested; on the contrary, when there are many low-frequency types, it may be expected that there are also types not yet attested.

6 Results

6.1 Memorization of words and part-words

First we analyze the effect of the different conditions (exposure time and presence of pauses) in the memorization of segments computed with R&R (step (i)). Figure 5 shows the presence of test items (the nine words and nine possible part-words) in the memory of R&R after different exposure times (average out of ten runs of the model). As can be seen, the subjective frequencies of part-words increase over time, and thus, the difference between words and part-words decreases as the exposure increases.

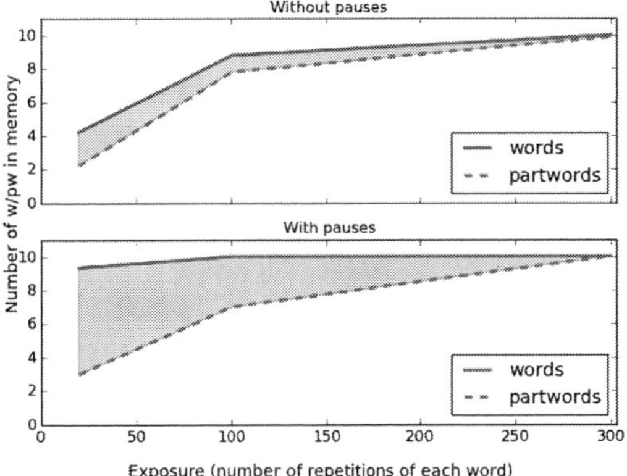

Figure 5: Average number of memorized words and part-words after familiarization with the stimuli in Peña et al., for 10 runs of the R&R model with an arbitrary parameter setting (A=0.5 B=0.5 C=0.2 D=0.5).

The graph also shows that, when the micropauses are present, words are readily identified after much less exposure, yielding clearer differences in subjective frequencies between words and part-words.

---

[2]It should be noticed that the reestimated probabilities need to be renormalized to sum up to 1, by multiplying with the estimated total probability of seen types $1 - P_0$ and dividing by the sum of unnormalized probabilites.

[3]SGT incorporates a rule for switching between N_r and $S(N_r)$ such that smoothed values $S(N_r)$ are only used when they yield significantly different results from N_r (when the difference is greater than 1.96 times the standard deviation).

The results of these simulations are consistent with the experimental results: the choice for words (or sequences generalized from words) against part-words should benefit from shorter exposures and from the presence of the micropauses. Now, given the subjective frequencies, how can we compute the propensity to generalize?

6.2 Prediction of observed decrease in the propensity to generalize

Next, we apply the Simple Good-Turing method [4] to subjective frequencies computed by the R&R model. As shown in figure 6, we find that the propensity to generalize (P_0) decreases as the exposure time increases, regardless of the parameter setting used in R&R. This result is consistent with the rationale in the Simple Good-Turing method: as exposure time increases, frequencies are shifted to greater values, causing a decrease in the smaller frequencies and therefore reducing the expectation for unattested sequences.

The results of these simulations point to a straightforward explanation of the experimental finding of a reduced preference for the generalized sequences: longer exposures repeat the same set of words (and partwords), and consequently, participants may conclude that there are no other sequences in that language – otherwise they would have probably appeared in such a long language sample.

It can be noticed in the graphs that the propensity to generalize is slightly smaller for the micropause condition. The reason for that is that R&R identifies words faster when micropauses are present, and therefore, the subjective frequencies tend to be greater. This might appear unexpected, but it is in fact not contradicting the empirical results: as shown in figure 5, the difference between words and partwords is much bigger in the condition with micropauses, so this effect is likely to override the small probability difference (as would be confirmed by a model of step (iii)). It should be noted that, as reported in Frost&Monaghan (2016), micropauses are not essential for all type of generalizations (as is evidenced with the fact that rule*-words are generalized in the no-pause condition). Like those authors, we see as the role of the micropauses to enhance the salience of initial and final syllables (A

---

[4]We use the free software implementation of Simple Good Turing in https://github.com/maxbane/simplegoodturing.

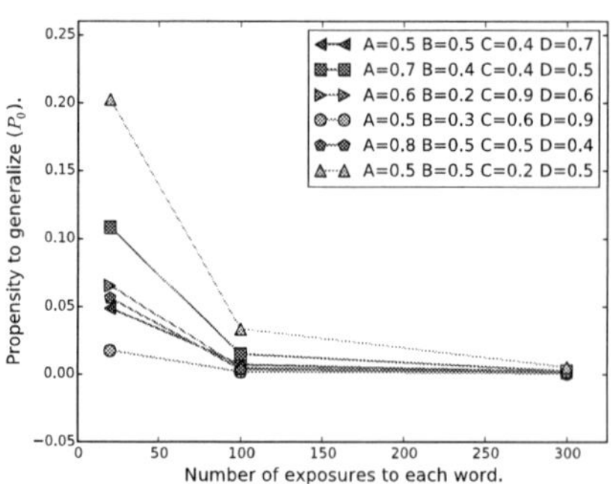

(a) Exposure without pauses.

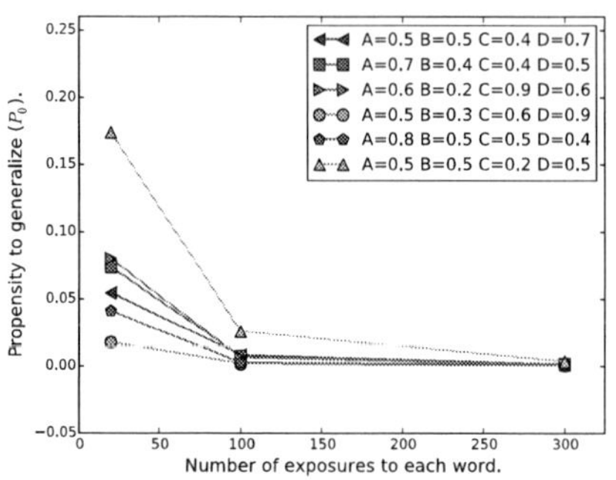

(b) Exposure with pauses.

Figure 6: Propensity to generalize, for several parameter settings (average of 100 runs). Our model shows a clear decrease for all parameter settings we tried, consistent with the empirical data (compare with figure 1).

and C) to compensate for the odd construction of the test items (rule-words and class-words), which include a middle syllable that occupied a different position in the familiarization stream.

7 Discussion

The experiments we have focused on are all based on the same simple language, but the results form a complex mosaic: generalization is observed in different degrees depending on the amount of exposure, the presence of micropauses and the type of generalization (rule-words, class-words or rule*-words). We have approached the analysis of these results with the use of several tools: first, with the 3-step approach, a conceptualization of generalization that identifies its main components; second, with the use of R&R, a probabilistic model that already predicts some aspects of the results —and, importantly, generates a skewed distribution of subjective frequencies that is crucial for step (ii); and third, with the Simple Good-Turing method for quantifying the propensity to generalize. We now discuss how we interpret the outcome of our study.

Framing generalization with the 3-step approach allowed us to identify a step that is usually neglected in discussion of ALL, namely, the computation of the propensity to generalize. We state that generalization is not only a process of discovering structure: the frequencies in the familiarization generate an expectation about the probability of next observing any unattested item, and the responses for generalized sequences must be affected by it. Moreover, this step is based on statistical information, proving that — contrary to the MoM hypothesis — a statistical mechanism can account for the negative correlation with exposure time.

It should be noted that our conclusion concerns the qualitative nature of the learning mechanism that is responsible for the experimental findings. It has been postulated that such findings evidence the presence of *multiple* mechanisms (Endress and Bonatti, 2016). In our view, the notion of 'mechanism' is only meaningful as a high-level construct that may help researchers in narrowing down the scope of the computations that are being studied, among all the computations that take place in the brain at a given time. After all, there is no natural obvious way to isolate the computations that would constitute a single 'mechanism', from an implementational point of view. Therefore, our 3-step approach should be taken as sketching the aspects that any model of generalization should account for, and our modelling efforts show that the experimental results are expected given the statistical properties of the input.

One issue to discuss is the influence of the use of the R&R model in computing the propensity to generalize. The Simple Good-Turing method is designed to exploit the fact that words in natural language follow a Zipfian distribution —that is, languages consist of a few highly frequent words and a long tail of unfrequent words. This is a key property of natural language that is normally violated in ALL experiments, since most of the artificial languages used are based on a uniform distribution of words (but see Kurumada et al. 2013). But it would be implausible to assume that subjects extract the exact distribution for an unknown artificial language to which they have been only briefly exposed. R&R models the transition from absolute to subjective frequencies, resulting in a distribution of subjective frequencies that shows a great degree of skew, and much more so than alternative models of segmentation in ALL. Thanks to this fact, the frequency distribution over which the SGT method operates (the subjective distribution) is more similar to that of natural language, and the pattern of results found for the propensity to generalize crucially depends on this type of distribution.

Finally, we have thus accomplished our goal qualitatively. We capture the downward tendency of the propensity to generalize, but a model for step (iii), a longstanding question in linguistics and cognitive science, is required to also achieve a quantitative fit. Developing a model of step (iii) is left as future work, but our approach already allowed us to propose concrete models of the first two steps, and explain much of the pattern of results.

Acknowledgments

This work was developed with Remko Scha, who sadly passed away before the finalization of this paper. We thank Carel ten Cate, Clara Levelt, Andreea Geambasu and Michelle Spierings for their feedback. We are also grateful to Raquel Fernández, Stella Frank and Miloš Stanojević for their comments on the paper. This research was funded by NWO (360-70-450).

References

Raquel G. Alhama, Remko Scha, and Willem Zuidema. 2016. Memorization of sequence-segments by humans and non-human animals: the retention-recognition model. *ILLC Prepublications*, PP-2016-08.

Richard N Aslin, Jenny R Saffran, and Elissa L Newport. 1998. Computation of conditional probability statistics by 8-month-old infants. *Psychological Science*, 9(4):321–324.

Noam Chomsky. 1957. *Syntactic Structures*. Mouton, The Hague.

A.D. Endress and L.L. Bonatti. 2007. Rapid learning of syllable classes from a perceptually continuous speech stream. *Cognition*, 105(2):247–299.

A.D. Endress and L.L. Bonatti. 2016. Words, rules, and mechanisms of language acquisition. *WIREs Cognitive Science*. (in press).

Robert M French and Garrison W Cottrell. 2014. Tracx 2.0: A memory-based, biologically-plausible model of sequence segmentation and chunk extraction. *Proceedings of the 36th Annual Conference of the Cognitive Science Society.*

Robert M. French, Caspar Addyman, and Denis Mareschal. 2011. Tracx: A recognition-based connectionist framework for sequence segmentation and chunk extraction. *Psychological Review*, 118(4):614.

Rebecca LA Frost and Padraic Monaghan. 2016. Simultaneous segmentation and generalisation of non-adjacent dependencies from continuous speech. *Cognition*, 147:70–74.

W. A. Gale and G. Sampson. 1995. Good-Turing frequency estimation without tears. *Journal of Quantitative Linguistics*, 2(3):217–237.

Sharon Goldwater, Thomas L Griffiths, and Mark Johnson. 2006. Contextual dependencies in unsupervised word segmentation. In *Proceedings of the annual meeting of the association for computational linguistics*, volume 44, pages 673–680.

Irwin J Good. 1953. The population frequencies of species and the estimation of population parameters. *Biometrika*, 40(3–4):237–264.

Marc D Hauser, Elissa L Newport, and Richard N Aslin. 2001. Segmentation of the speech stream in a non-human primate: Statistical learning in cotton-top tamarins. *Cognition*, 78(3):B53–B64.

G.F. Marcus, S. Vijayan, S.B. Rao, and P.M. Vishton. 1999. Rule learning by seven-month-old infants. *Science*, 283(5398):77–80.

L. Onnis, P. Monaghan, K. Richmond, and N. Chater. 2005. Phonology impacts segmentation in online speech processing. *Journal of Memory and Language*, 53(2):225–237.

Fernando Pereira. 2000. Formal grammar and information theory: Together again? *Philosophical Transactions of the Royal Society*, 358(1769):1239–1253.

Pierre Perruchet and Annie Vinter. 1998. Parser: A model for word segmentation. *Journal of Memory and Language*, 39(2):246–263.

M. Peña, L.L. Bonatti, M. Nespor, and J. Mehler. 2002. Signal-driven computations in speech processing. *Science*, 298(5593):604–607.

Steven Pinker and Alan Prince. 1988. On language and connectionism: Analysis of a parallel distributed processing model of language acquisition. *Cognition*, 28:73–193.

D.E. Rumelhart and J.L. McClelland. 1986. On learning past tenses of English verbs. In D.E. Rumelhart and J.L. McClelland, editors, *Parallel Distributed Processing, Vol. 2*, pages 318–362. MIT Press, Cambridge, MA.

Jenny R Saffran, Richard N Aslin, and Elissa L Newport. 1996a. Statistical learning by 8-month-old infants. *Science*, 274(5294):1926–1928.

Jenny R Saffran, Elissa L Newport, and Richard N Aslin. 1996b. Word segmentation: the role of distributional cues. *Journal of Memory and Language*, 35(4):606–621.

Mark S Seidenberg and Jeffrey L Elman. 1999. Networks are not 'hidden rules'. *Trends in Cognitive Sciences*, 3(8):288–289.

Juan M. Toro and Josep B. Trobalón. 2005. Statistical computations over a speech stream in a rodent. *Perception & Psychophysics*, 67(5):867–875.

Explicit Causal Connections between the Acquisition of Linguistic Tiers: Evidence from Dynamical Systems Modeling

Daniel Spokoyny and **Jeremy Irvin**
College of Creative Studies
University of California, Santa Barbara
Santa Barbara, CA 93106, USA
dspoka@gmail.com
jirvin@umail.ucsb.edu

Fermín Moscoso del Prado Martín
Department of Linguistics
University of California, Santa Barbara
Santa Barbara, CA 93106, USA
fmoscoso@linguistics.ucsb.edu

Abstract

In this study, we model the *causal* links between the complexities of different macroscopic aspects of child language. We consider pairs of sequences of measurements of the quantity and diversity of the lexical and grammatical properties. Each pair of sequences is taken as the trajectory of a high-dimensional dynamical system, some of whose dimensions are unknown. We use Multispatial Convergent Cross Mapping to ascertain the directions of causality between the pairs of sequences. Our results provide support for the hypothesis that children learn grammar through distributional learning, where the generalization of smaller structures enables generalizations at higher levels, consistent with the proposals of construction-based approaches to language.

1 Introduction

A crucial question in language acquisition concerns how (or, according to some, whether) children learn the grammars of their native languages. Some researchers, mainly coming from the generative tradition, argue that, although the grammatical rules are possibly 'innate' (e.g., Pinker, 1994), children still need to learn how to map the different semantic/grammatical roles onto the different options offered by Universal Grammar (e.g., 'parameter-setting'). The evidence, however, does not seem to support this hypothesis. For instance, Bowerman (1990) notes that the type of semantic aspects learned by the child do not match well into the prototypical roles that would be required to map into hard linguistic rules (e.g., learning an AGENT category to map onto the SUBJECT syntactic role). Other researchers (e.g., Goldberg, 2003;

Tomasello, 1992; Tomasello, 2005) propose that there is a gradual increase in the generality of the structures learned by the child, which are slowly acquired through distributional learning. Such a picture is strongly supported by the remarkably little creativity exhibited by children, most of whose utterances are often literal repetitions of those that they have previously heard (Lieven et al., 1997; Pine and Lieven, 1993), with little or no generalization in the early stages. It appears as though children progressively and conservatively increase the level at which they generalize linguistic constructions, building from the words upwards, in what some have termed 'lexically-based positional analysis' (Lieven et al., 1997).

The Theory of Dynamical Systems offers powerful tools for modeling human development (e.g, Smith and Thelen, 2003; van Geert, 1991). It provides a mathematical framework for implementing the principle that development involves the mutual and continuous interaction of multiple levels of the developing system, which simultaneously unfold over many time-scales. Typically, a dynamical system is described by a system of coupled differential equations governing the temporal evolution of multiple parts of the system and their interrelations. One difficulty that arises when trying to model a dynamical system as complex as the development of language is that many factors that are important for the evolution of the system might not be available or might not be easily measurable or –even worse– there are additional variables relevant for the system of which the modeler is not even aware. In this respect, a crucial development was the discovery that, in a deterministic coupled dynamical system –even in the presence of noise– the dynamics of the whole system can be satisfactorily recovered using measurements of a single of the system's variables (Takens' Embedding Theorem; Takens, 1981).

73

Proceedings of the 7th Workshop on Cognitive Aspects of Computational Language Learning, pages 73–81,
Berlin, Germany, August 11, 2016. ©2016 Association for Computational Linguistics

The finding above opens an interesting avenue for understanding the processes involved in language acquisition. In the same way that systems of differential equations can be used to model the evolution of ecosystems (e.g., predator-prey systems), one could take measurements of the detailed properties of child language, and build a detailed system of equations capturing the macroscopic dynamics of the process. However, in order to achieve this, it is necessary to ascertain the ways in which different measured variables in the system affect each other. This problem goes beyond estimating correlations (as could be obtained, for instance, using regression models), as one needs to detect asymmetrical *causal* relations between the variables of interest, so that these causal influences can be incorporated into the models.

In this study, we investigate the causal relations different macroscopic-level measures characterizing the level of development of different tiers child language (i.e., number of words produced, lexical diversity, inflectional diversity and mean length of utterances), using the longitudinal data provided in the Manchester Corpus (Theakston et al., 2001). In order to detect causal relations between the different measures, we make use of state space reconstruction relying on Takens (1981)'s Embedding Theorem, and recently developed techniques for assessing the strength of causal relations in dynamical systems (Multispatial Convergent Cross Mapping; Clark et al., 2015). Here, we provide a detailed picture of the causal connections between the development of different aspects of a child's language (while acquiring English). Our result provide support for theories that advocate distributional learning of linguistic constructions by gradual generalizations from the level of words to larger scale constructions.

2 Causality Detection in Dynamical Systems

Whenever two variables are correlated, there *must* exist some causal link between them. Namely, if variables A and B are found to be correlated, then one of four possibilities must be true: (a) A causes B, (b) B causes A, (c) A and B form a feedback loop, each causing the other, or (d) there is a third variable C causing both A and B. For studying the interactions of species within ecosystems, Sugihara et al. (2012) introduced *Convergent Cross Mapping* (CCM), a causality-detection technique

that is valid for non-separable systems, is capable of identifying weakly coupled variables even in the presence of noise, and –crucially– can distinguish direct causal relations between variables from effects of shared driving variables (i.e., in possibility (d) above, CCM would *not* find causality).

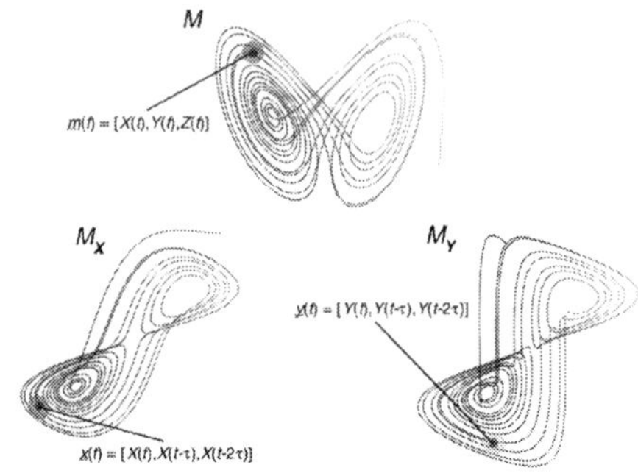

Figure 1: Reconstructed manifold for Lorenz's system (M; top), as well as the shadow manifolds reconstructed considering only X (M_X; bottom-left) and Y (M_Y; bottom-right) (reprinted with permission from Sugihara et al., 2012).

For instance, consider E. Lorenz's often studied dynamical system, which includes three coupled variables $X(t)$, $Y(t)$, and $Z(t)$ whose coevolution is described by the system of differential equations

$$\begin{cases} \dfrac{\mathrm{d}X}{\mathrm{d}t} = \sigma(Y - X) \\ \dfrac{\mathrm{d}Y}{\mathrm{d}t} = X(\rho - Z) - Y \\ \dfrac{\mathrm{d}Z}{\mathrm{d}t} = XY - \beta Z \end{cases} \tag{1}$$

The first equation in this system indicates that there is a relation by which Y causes X, as the change in X (i.e., its future value) depends on the value of Y (i.e., the future of X depends on the past of Y even after the past of X itself has been considered), a causal relation whose strength is indexed by parameter σ. The manifold defined by these three variables (Lorenz's famous strange attractor), which we can denote by M, is plotted in the top of Fig. 1. In many circumstances, however, not all variables of the system are available (some might be difficult to measure, or we might not even be aware of their relevance). It is at this point that Takens (1981)'s Embedding Theorem comes into play. Informally speaking, the theorem states that the properties of a coupled dynamical system's attractor can be recovered using only measurements from a single one of its variables. This is achieved by considering multiple versions of the same variable lagged in time, that is, instead of plotting $(X[t], Y[t], Z[t])$, when only measurements of X are available, we can plot $(X[t], X[t+\tau], \ldots, X[t+(E-1)\tau])$. These reconstructed manifolds are termed "shadow" manifolds. M_X denotes the shadow manifold of M reconstructed on the basis of X alone. There are well-studied techniques for finding the appropriate values for the parameters for the lag τ and the number of dimensions E (c.f., Abarbanel et al., 1993) so that the properties of the original manifold M are recovered by the shadow manifold M_X. Fig. 1 illustrates this point by plotting the shadow manifolds M_X (bottom-left) and M_Y (bottom-right) for the Lorenz system. Notice how both shadow manifolds recover much of the original's structure, using only knowledge of one of its three variables.

Each point in the original manifold M maps onto points in its shadow manifolds, as is illustrated by the points labelled $m(t)$, $x(t)$, and $y(t)$ in Fig. 1. The preservation of the topological properties of the original manifold in its shadow manifolds entails that points that are close-by in the original manifold will also be close-by in its shadow versions. This implies that, for causally linked variables within the same dynamical system, the state of one variable can identify the states of the others. Sugihara et al. (2012) noticed that, when one variable X stochastically drives another variable Y, information about the states of X can be recovered from Y, but not vice-versa. This is the basic insight of the CCM method. To test for causality from X to Y, CCM looks for the signature of X in Y's time series by seeing whether the time indices of nearby points on M_Y can be used to identify nearby points on M_X. Crucially, in order to distinguish causation from mere correlation, CCM requires *convergence*, that is, that cross-mapped estimates improve in estimation accuracy with the sample size (i.e., "library size") used for reconstructing the manifolds. As the library size increases, the trajectories defining the manifolds fill in, resulting in closer nearest neighbors and declining estimation error, which is reflected in a higher correlation coefficient between the points in the neighborhoods of the shadow manifolds. Con-

vergence then becomes the necessary condition for inferring causation. Using both artificial systems and ecological time-series with known dynamics, Sugihara and his colleagues demonstrated that this technique successfully recovers true directional causal relations when these are present, and –crucially– is able to discard spurious causation in the case when both variables are causally driven by a third, unknown, variable, but there is no true direct causation between them.

An inconvenience of CCM, and in general of techniques that rely on manifold reconstruction, is that they generally require that relatively long time-series of the behavior of the system are available. Such long series are, however, very difficult, if not impossible, to obtain in many fields, including of course language acquisition. One can however obtain multiple short time series from different instances of a similar dynamical system. In ecology, for instance, one can obtain short sequences of measurements of the population densities of a group of species measured at different places and times. In language acquisition, we might have multiple, relatively short longitudinal sequences of measurements from different children. With this in mind Clark et al. (2015) developed Multispatial CCM (mCCM), an extension of CCM able to infer causal relations from multiple short time-series measured at different sites, making use of dewdrop regression (Hsieh et al., 2008) to take the additional heterogeneity into account.

3 Materials and Methods

3.1 Materials

We obtained from the CHILDES database (MacWhinney, 2000) the transcriptions contained in the Manchester Corpus (Theakston et al., 2001). This corpus contains annotated transcripts of audio recordings from a longitudinal study of 12 British English-speaking children (6 girls and 6 boys) between the ages of approximately two and three years. The children were recorded at their homes for an hour while they engaged in normal play activities with their mothers. Each child was recorded on two separate occasions in every three-week period for one year. Each recording session is divided into two half-hour periods. The annotations include the lemmatized form of the words produced by the children (incomplete words and small word-internal errors were manually corrected in the lemmatization).

In order to increase the sample size in each period, we followed a sliding window technique of (Irvin et al., in press): We computed measures for the samples contained in overlapping windows of three consecutive corpus files. In this way, at each point we obtained samples originating from two files from the same recording session, and a file from either the previous or the next recording session.

3.2 Measures of Linguistic Development

As in previous studies (Irvin et al., in press; Moscoso del Prado Martín, in press), in order to measure the overall amount of speech produced by each child, we counted the total number of word tokens produced by each child in each temporal window. We refer to this measure as the child's *loquacity*.

In order to measure the diversity of the words used by the children, we use the *lexical diversity* measure (Irvin et al., in press; Moscoso del Prado Martín, in press). This is just the information entropy (Shannon, 1948) of the probability distribution of word lemmas found in the sample,

$$ H[L] = \sum_{\ell \in L} \mathrm{p}(\ell) \cdot \log \frac{1}{\mathrm{p}(\ell)}, \qquad (2) $$

where L refers to the set of word lemmas found in a sample, and $\mathrm{p}(\ell)$ is the probability with which the particular lemma ℓ is found in that sample. Entropy estimates obtained using Eq. 2 using maximum likelihood estimates of the probabilities are known to be strongly biased (Miller, 1955), with the bias magnitude correlating with the size of the sample used. Importantly, the sample size is nothing else than the loquacity measure described above. Therefore, using this plain maximum likelihood method would result in spurious correlations. For this reason, Moscoso del Prado Martín (in press) recommends using the bias-adjusted entropy estimator (Chao et al., 2013, see Appendix A) instead of Eq. 2.

In order to measure the acquisition of inflectional morphological paradigms, we make use of the *inflectional diversity* measure (Moscoso del Prado Martín, in press). This is a macroscopic generalization of inflectional entropy (Moscoso del Prado Martín et al., 2004), a measure that is known to index morphological influences on adult lexical processing (Baayen and Moscoso del Prado Martín, 2005; Moscoso del Prado Martín et al., 2004) as well as in child language acquisition (Stoll et al., 2012). The inflectional entropy of a lemma ℓ ($H[W|\ell]$) is the information entropy of the inflected variants of that lemma. Our inflectional diversity is just the average value of inflectional entropy across all lemmas,

$$ H[W|L] = H[W, L] - H[L], \qquad (3) $$

where $H[L]$ is the lexical diversity measure described above, and $H[W, L]$ is the joint entropy between the inflected word forms and their corresponding lemmas,

$$ H[W, L] = \sum_{\ell \in L} \sum_{w \in W} \mathrm{p}(w, \ell) \cdot \log \frac{1}{\mathrm{p}(w, \ell)}, \qquad (4) $$

where L denotes the set of all distinct lemmas encountered in the sample, W is the set of all distinct inflected word forms encountered, and $\mathrm{p}(w, \ell)$ is the joint probability with which lemma ℓ occurs as the specific inflected form w. Inflectional diversity takes non-negative values, measuring how large are the average inflectional paradigms used in the language sample. Estimating $H[W, L]$ using Eq. 4 is subject to the same estimation biases that were described for lexical diversity. Therefore, we also follow Moscoso del Prado Martín (in press) in using the bias-adjusted estimate (Chao et al., 2013, see Appendix A) for this magnitude, and then combining it with the lexical diversity using Eq. 3 to obtain our inflectional diversity estimates.

Finally, in order to measure the degree of syntactic development of the children we used their *mean length of utterances* (MLU). Instead of measuring MLU in morphemes (Brown, 1973), we used the simpler, but equally accurate measure in number of words (c.f., Parker and Bronson, 2005). In these ages, MLUs are well known to provide an accurate measure of the syntactic richness of the utterances produced (Brown, 1973), and in fact correlate almost perfectly with explicit measurements of grammatical diversity (Moscoso del Prado Martín, in press).

3.3 Reconstruction of Shadow Manifolds

Using the windowing technique, for each child we obtained four time series, one corresponding to each of the four measures described above: loquacity, lexical diversity, inflectional diversity, and MLU. These time series are plotted in Fig. 2

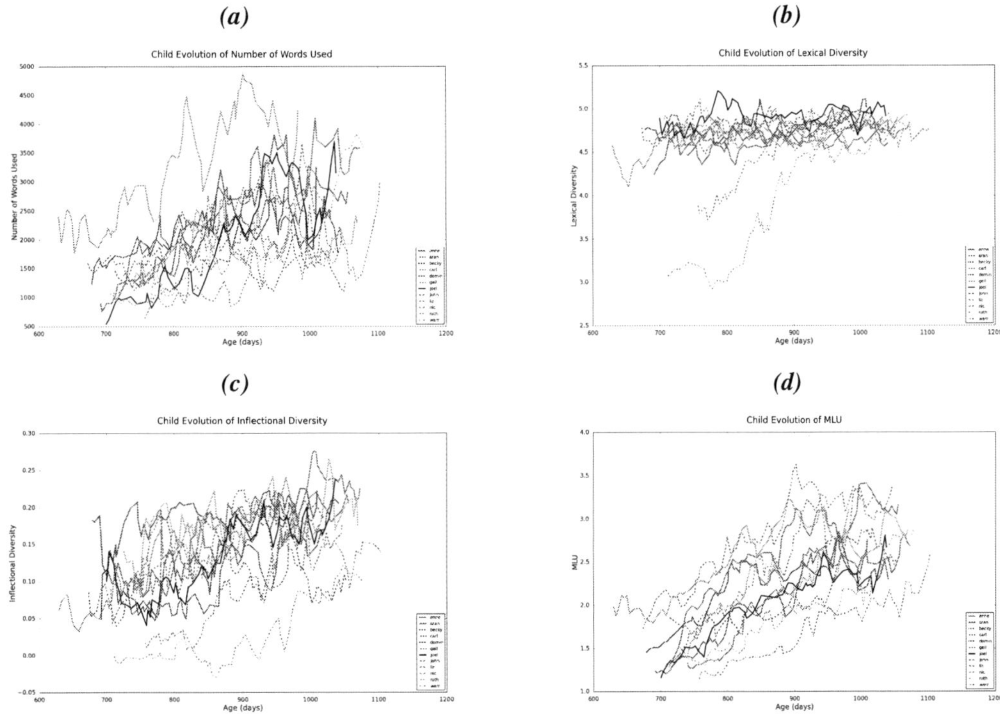

Figure 2: Evolution of the measures studied as a function of the children's ages (in days). *(a)* Evolution of the loquacity (measured in number of word tokens produced) for each of the twelve children. *(b)* Evolution of the lexical diversity (measured in nats per word) for each of the twelve children. *(c)* Evolution of the inflectional diversity (measured in nats per word) for each of the twelve children. *(d)* Evolution of the MLU (in number of words per utterance) for each of the twelve children.

Parameter	Loquacity	Lexical Diversity	Inflectional Diversity	MLU
τ	3	2	3	3
E	3	3	2	4

Table 1: Parameter values used in the reconstruction of the shadow attractors based on each of the four measures.

In order to ensure that applying the non-linear dynamics techniques on these time series was sensible, the series were checked to ensure that they contained non-linear signal not dominated by noise. This was achieved using a prediction test (Clark et al., 2015): We ensured that, for all four variables, the ability to predict future values significantly decreased as one increases the distance in the future at which the predictions are being made. This increasing unpredictability is the hallmark of non-linear dynamical systems. Therefore, we could safely proceed to reconstruct the shadow attractors.

Following Clark et al. (2015), we reconstructed the shadow attractors from each of these collections of time series. The optimal time-lags (τ) for constructing the shadow manifolds were estimated as the first local minimum of the lagged self-information in each of the time series (c.f., Abarbanel et al., 1993). The optimal embedding dimensionalities (E) were estimated by optimizing next-step prediction accuracy. The estimates were not found to differ significantly across children, and therefore for each measure, we used a single estimate of (τ, E) for all children. The estimated optimal parameter values used for the reconstruction of each shadow attractor are given in Table 1.

3.4 Detection of Causal Relationships

The presence of directional causal relations was tested for each of the six possible pairs of variables using mCCM. We performed 1,000 bootstrapping iterations for assessing the p-values of the relations.[1] Finally, to account for our lack of *a priori* predictions on the causal directions to be tested, the p-values were adjusted for multiple comparisons using the false discovery rate procedure for correlated data (FDR; Benjamini and Yekutieli, 2001).

4   Results

As plotted in Fig. 2, the four groups of time-series considered here exhibit different patterns of development. On the one hand, the loquacity, inflectional diversity, and MLU series show evidence of a more or less linear increase along the child's development, with their values towards the end of the studied interval being close to what was found for their mothers in those same conversations. On the other hand, the lexical diversity measure exhibits quite constant patterns across all children, with their values being pretty much indistinguishable from those observed for their mothers. This latter pattern is slighly different in two chilren (Ruth and Nick), who seem to be experiencing their 'vocabulary burst' later than the rest of the children did. In fact, if one examines panel *(c)* in detail, one sees that the inflectional diversity curves for these two children only begin their linear increases *after* the children have experienced their vocabulary bursts. A similar pattern can be seen in the MLU curves (panel *(d)*) for these two particular children, with syntactic development apparently being delayed by their late vocabulary bursts. These two patterns suggest that the development of both grammatical components of their language (inflectional morphology and syntax) depends on having attained a certain degree of vocabulary richness. However, just examining these curves does not provide explicit evidence on whether these hypothesized causal relationships are actually reliable ones or they are just statistical mirages. The mCCM method addresses such question directly.

Fig. 3 plots the results of mCCM for each pair of reconstructed shadow manifolds. The curves plot how the correlations between nearest neighbors across shadow attractors evolve as one considers increasingly larger library sizes. The p-values report whether these correlation values are significantly increasing (the p-values are obtained by a Monte Carlo method with 1,000 resamplings, and further corrected for the twelve comparisons using

the FDR procedure).

Using the p-values in Fig. 3 enables the reconstruction of the network of causal relations depicted in Fig. 4. In this graph, the causal relation between the loquacity and the lexical diversity is considered weaker than the rest. The reason for this is that the comparisons reported here are in fact part of a larger study considering many more comparisons (including many factors of the mothers as well), on which we did not have any clear *a priori* predictions on the relations that would be found. When applying the FDR method on the whole set of 56 comparisons that we actually considered, the relation plotted by the dashed arrow is in fact not significant. In short, one should not trust the reliability of that particular relation.

Considering only the fully reliable relations, one finds that, as was suspected from the curves in Fig. 2, there is an explicit causal relation between the development of vocabulary richness (i.e., lexical diversity) and the acquisition of inflectional paradigms (i.e., inflectional diversity). The increase in lexical diversity indeed *causes* the development of inflectional paradigms. In turn, that the inflectional paradigms begin to be in place enables the child to begin generalizing more syntactic relationships (as is reflected by the feedback loop found between the inflectional diversity and MLU manifolds). Importantly, that the inflectional paradigms are developed is also strongly coupled (i.e., forms a feedback loop) with the increase the children's overall loquacity; once children begin to get a hold of grammar (inflection and syntax) they are enabled to speak more, which in turn furthers their ability to generalize morphological relations and –by association– syntactic relations.

5   Discussion

In this study, we have –for the first time– documented the explicit *causal* relations between different tiers of children's linguistic development. At a macroscopic level, we find strictly causal relations between the acquisition of vocabulary, inflectional paradigms, and syntactic relationships. As schematized in Fig. 4, the development of a sufficiently large vocabulary is a crucial trigger for the successful acquisition of the grammatical aspects of language, which are in turn necessary for children to be able to speak more. These results are consistent with theories advocating the importance distributional learning for the acqui-

---

[1] All computations were done using R package `multispatialCCM` (Clark et al., 2015).

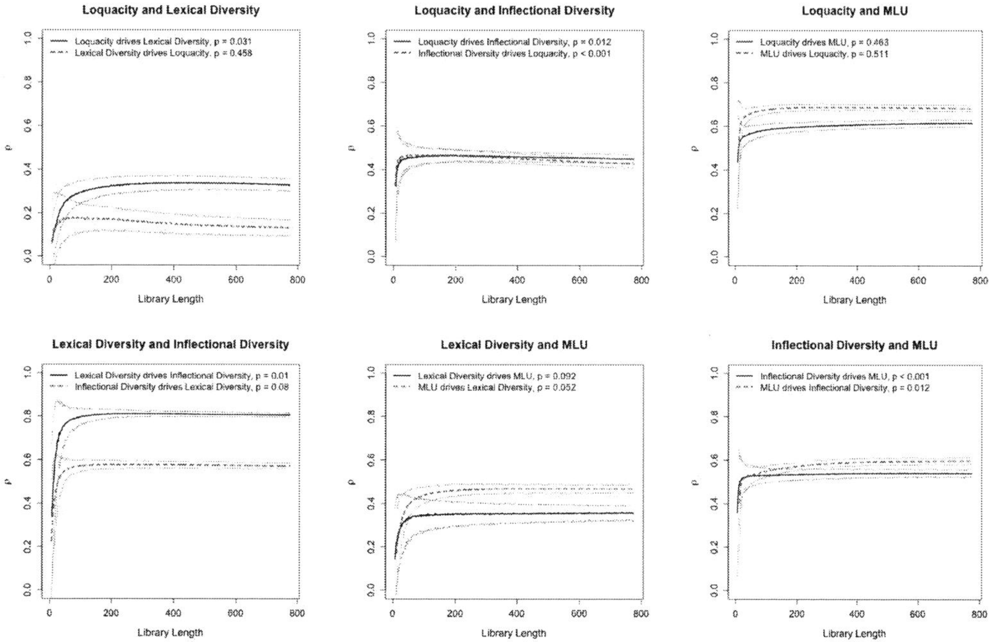

Figure 3: Results of mCCM between each pair of variables. The *p*-values are FDR-corrected considering the twelve comparisons reported here.

sition of constructions (Lieven et al., 1997; Pine and Lieven, 1993; Tomasello, 1992; Tomasello, 2005). It shows how the level of generality of the constructions is progressively increased (Goldberg, 2003) by the use of 'lexically-based positional analysis' (Lieven et al., 1997) to achieve early grammatical generalizations.

The picture of causal relations observed here could be put into an informal narrative as follows: The acquisition of sufficient lexical forms enables children to generalize their relations into inflectional paradigms. When a sufficient command of the language's inflectional morphology has arisen, children are able to begin generalizing syntactic relations. The presence of these early syntactic developments in turn serves to increase the child's awareness of the functional roles served by different paradigm members. From this point, one observes the strong bidirectional coupling between the development of syntax and inflectional morphology. An increasing awareness of the functional roles of the individual forms within these paradigms, and noticing the formal relations between them, in turn trigger further generalizations of the paradigms into *inflectional classes* (Milin et al., 2009), further increasing the productivity of the inflectional morphology system.

This study also stresses the importance of *macroscopic* level linguistic analyses. Whereas much research in language acquisition has focused on the acquisition of specific individual constructions (*microscopic* level) or groups thereof (*mesoscopic* level), the investigation of the properties of the whole lexicon, inflectional and syntactic systems uncovers relations which are difficult to pinpoint at the other levels. This fits in well with the multiscale investigation of language development proposed from the point of view of the Theory of Dynamical Systems (van Geert, 1991). Indeed, one can see, at the mesoscopic level, that –also consistent with the distributional learning hypothesis– there is a causal chain by which the development of single word utterances triggers the development of two-word utterances, which in turn trigger three-word utterances, and so forth (Bassano and van Geert, 2007). The macroscopic analyses provided here complement that picture by indicating how that evolution of utterance lengths is strongly coupled with the development (or 'growth' in van Geert's terms) of grammatical knowledge.

An innovative aspect of the methods we have developed in this paper is that they provide an explicit procedure for testing whether there are ex-

79

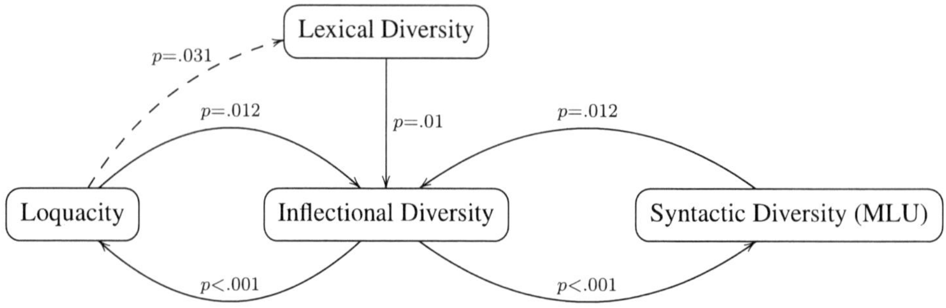

Figure 4: Reconstructed network of causal relations between the different measures of the children's linguistic performances. The p-values indicated on the causal arrows are FDR-corrected. The dashed-line denotes a relationship that does not survive FDR correction considering a larger set of variables.

plicit causal relations between the development of different aspects of language. Here we have used the methods at a macroscopic level, but it would be equally possible to apply them to both microscopic- or mesoscopic-level time series. Previous research on dynamical systems on language acquisition (e.g., Bassano and van Geert, 2007; Steenbeek and van Geert, 2007; van Geert, 1991) relies on proposing different candidate models in terms of systems of differential equations, each including different sets of causal relations and couplings between time series. Our methods, using techniques for explicitly testing causal relations borrowed from ecology (a field whose study bears uncanny similarities with the study of human development), complement the curve-fitting by explicitly testing which couplings and causalities should be included in the models, thus significantly reducing the model space that needs to be explored.

References

Henry D. I. Abarbanel, Reggie Brown, John J. Sidorowich, and Lev Sh. Tsimring. 1993. The analysis of observed chaotic data in physical systems. *Reviews of Modern Physics*, 65:1331–1392.

R. Harald Baayen and Fermín Moscoso del Prado Martín. 2005. Semantic density and past-tense formation in three Germanic languages. *Language*, 81:666–698.

Dominique Bassano and Paul L. C. van Geert. 2007. Modeling continuity and discontinuity in utterance length: a quantitative approach to changes, transitions and intraindividual variability in early grammatical development. *Developmental Science*, 10:588–512.

Yoav Benjamini and Daniel Yekutieli. 2001. The control of the false discovery rate in multiple testing under dependency. *Annals of Statistics*, 29:1165–1188.

Melissa Bowerman. 1990. Mapping thematic roles onto syntactic functions: are children helped by innate linking rules? *Linguistics*, 28:1253–1289.

Roger Brown. 1973. *A first language: the early stages*. Harvard University Press, Cambridge, MA.

Anne Chao, Y. T. Wang, and Lou Jost. 2013. Entropy and the species accumulation curve: a novel entropy estimator via discovery rates of new species. *Methods in Ecology and Evolution*, 4:1091–1100.

Adam Thomas Clark, Hao Ye, Forest Isbell, Ethan R. Deyle, Jane Cowles, G. David Tilman, and George Sugihara. 2015. Spatial convergent cross mapping to detect causal relationships from short time series. *Ecology*, 96:1174–1181.

Adele E. Goldberg. 2003. Constructions: a new theoretical approach to language. *TRENDS in Cognitive Sciences*, 7:219–224.

Chih-hao Hsieh, Christian Anderson, and George Sugihara. 2008. Extending nonlinear analysis to short ecological time series. *The American Naturalist*, 171:71–80.

Jeremy Irvin, Daniel Spokoyny, and Fermín Moscoso del Prado Martín. in press. Dynamical systems modeling of the child–mother dyad: Causality between child-directed language complexity and language development. In Anna Papafragou, John Trueswell, Dan Grodner, and Dan Mirman, editors, *Proceedings of the 38th Annual Conference of the Cognitive Science Society*. Cognitive Science Society, Austin, TX.

Elena V. M. Lieven, Julian M. Pine, and Gilliam Baldwin. 1997. Lexically-based learning and early grammatical development. *Journal of Child Language*, 24:187–219.

Brian MacWhinney. 2000. *The CHILDES Project: Tools for analyzing talk*, volume 2: The database. Lawrence Erlbaum Associates, Mahwah, NJ, 3rd edition.

Petar Milin, Dušica Filipović Ðurđević, and Fermín Moscoso del Prado Martín. 2009. The simultaneous effects of inflectional paradigms and classes on lexical recognition: Evidence from Serbian. *Journal of Memory and Language*, 60:50–64.

George Miller. 1955. Note on the bias of information estimates. In Henry Quastler, editor, *Information Theory in Psychology: Problems and Methods*, pages 95–100. Free Press, Glencoe, IL.

Fermín Moscoso del Prado Martín, Aleksandar Kostić, and R. Harald Baayen. 2004. Putting the bits together: an information theoretical perspective on morphological processing. *Cognition*, 94:1–18.

Fermín Moscoso del Prado Martín. in press. Vocabulary, grammar, sex, and aging. *Cognitive Science*.

Matthew D. Parker and Kent Brorson. 2005. A comparative study between mean length of utterance in morphemes (MLUm) and mean length of utterance in words (MLUw). *First Language*, 25:365–376.

Julian M. Pine and Elena V. M. Lieven. 1993. Reanalysing rote-learned phrases: individual differences in the transition to multiword speech. *Journal of Child Language*, 20:43–60.

Steven Pinker. 1994. *The language instinct: How the mind creates language*. Harper-Collins, New York, NY.

Claude E. Shannon. 1948. A mathematical theory of communication. *The Bell System Technical Journal*, 27:379–423, 623–656.

Linda Smith and Esther Thelen. 2003. Development as a dynamic system. *TRENDS in Cognitive Sciences*, 7:343–348.

Hederien W. Steenbeek and Paul L. C. van Geert. 2007. A theory and dynamic model of dyadic interaction: Concerns, appraisals, and contagiousness in a developmental context. *Developmental Review*, 27:1–40.

Sabine Stoll, Bathasar Bickel, Elena Lieven, Netra P. Paudyal, Goma Banjade, Toya N. Bhatta, Martin Gaenszle, Judith Pettigrew, Ichchha Purna Rai, Manoj Rai, and Novel Kishore Rai. 2012. Nouns and verbs in Chintang: Children's usage and surrounding adult speech. *Journal of Child Language*, 39:284–321.

George Sugihara, Robert May, Hao Ye, Chih-hao Hsieh, Ethan R. Deyle, Michael Fogarty, and Stephan Munch. 2012. Detecting causality in complex ecosystems. *Science*, 338:496–500.

Floris Takens. 1981. Detecting strange attractors in turbulence. In D. A. Rand and L.-S. Young, editors, *Dynamical Systems and Turbulence*, pages 366–381. Springer Verlag, Berlin, Germany.

Anna L. Theakston, Elena V. M. Lieven, Julian M. Pine, and Caroline F. Rowland. 2001. The role of performance limitations in the acquisition of verb-argument structure: an alternative account. *Journal of Child Language*, 28:127–152.

Michael Tomasello. 1992. *First Verbs: a Case Study of Early Grammatical Development*. Cambridge University Press, Cambridge, England.

Michael Tomasello. 2005. Beyond formalities: The case of language acquisition. *The Linguistic Review*, 22:183–197.

Paul L. C. van Geert. 1991. A dynamic systems model of cognitive and language growth. *Psychological Review*, 98:3–53.

A   Bias-Adjusted Entropy Estimator

The bias-adjusted entropy estimator (Chao et al., 2013) relies on properties of the accumulation curve of the number of distinct words observed (i.e., the species accumulation curve in the biological terms of the original paper). The estimator is given by

$$\hat{H} = \sum_{1 \leq F_i \leq n-1} \left[\frac{F_i}{n} \left(\sum_{k=F_i}^{n-1} \frac{1}{k} \right) \right] - \frac{f_1}{n}(1-A)^{1-n} \left[\log(A) + \sum_{r=1}^{n-1} \frac{1}{r}(1-A)^r \right],$$

where F_i are the word frequencies observed in the sample, n is the number of tokens in the corpus, and

$$A = \begin{cases} \dfrac{2f_2}{(n-1)f_1 + 2f_2} & \text{if } f_2 > 0, \\[2ex] \dfrac{2}{(n-1)(f_1-1)+2} & \text{if } f_2 = 0, f_1 > 0, \\[2ex] 1 & \text{if } f_1 = f_2 = 0, \end{cases}$$

with f_1 and f_2 being the number of word types that were encountered exactly once or twice respectively (i.e., the numbers of *hapax legomena* and *dis legomena*). This estimator is demonstrated to be accurate and unbiased for word frequency distributions (Moscoso del Prado Martín, in press).

Modelling the informativeness and timing of non-verbal cues in parent–child interaction

Kristina Nilsson Björkenstam[1], Mats Wirén[1] and Robert Östling[2]
{kristina.nilsson, mats.wiren}@ling.su.se, robert.ostling@helsinki.fi

[1]Department of Linguistics
Stockholm University
SE-106 91 Stockholm, Sweden

[2]Department of Modern Languages
University of Helsinki
PL 24 (Unionsgatan 40)
00014 Helsinki, Finland

Abstract

How do infants learn the meanings of their first words? This study investigates the informativeness and temporal dynamics of non-verbal cues that signal the speaker's referent in a model of early word–referent mapping. To measure the information provided by such cues, a supervised classifier is trained on information extracted from a multimodally annotated corpus of 18 videos of parent–child interaction with three children aged 7 to 33 months. Contradicting previous research, we find that gaze is the single most informative cue, and we show that this finding can be attributed to our fine-grained temporal annotation. We also find that offsetting the timing of the non-verbal cues reduces accuracy, especially if the offset is negative. This is in line with previous research, and suggests that synchrony between verbal and non-verbal cues is important if they are to be perceived as causally related.

1 Background and introduction

There is a growing literature on how infants use non-verbal input such as parents' hand manipulations of salient objects to infer the meanings of their first words. Meaning seems to arise as a probabilistic process where recurrent acoustic patterns gain referential value as they are linked to time-synchronous recurrent patterns in other modalities (Trueswell et al., 2016; Gogate et al., 2006; Matatyaho and Gogate, 2008; Lacerda, 2009). The details of this process, such as the informativeness and temporal dynamics

of different cues in word–referent mapping, are still contested, though. In the social-pragmatic approach, joint attention and understanding of speakers' communicative intentions are the central vehicle for investigating the mapping, but the mechanisms typically appear to be deterministic (Tomasello, 2000). In contrast, the associative learning approach emphasises how cross-situational co-occurrences of words and referents increase the salience of objects, including multiple objects in ambiguous learning contexts.

A frequently used methodology for studying word–referent mapping is the Human Simulation Paradigm (HSP), originally devised by Gleitman and colleagues (Gillette et al., 1999; Piccin and Waxman, 2007; Medina et al., 2011). Here, observers try to estimate referential transparency by reconstructing intended referents from non-verbal cues as they watch a muted video of parent–child interaction. Another methodology, which is used in this paper, is to try to model the word–referent mapping directly. Such a model is based on coding of the referential events in a video, typically as perceived by an ideal observer (Geisler, 2011); in other words, someone assumed to optimally handle the perceptual task given by the learning environment as a whole, as recorded by the video. An example of this line of work is Yu and Ballard (2007). They combined social cues (in the form of prosodic affect and joint attention) with statistical learning of cross-situational co-occurrence into a unified model of word learning, showing that this model performed better than a purely statistical approach. Furthermore, Frank et al. (2009) showed that a unified model of cross-situational co-occurrence and interpretation of speakers' referential intention out-

Proceedings of the 7th Workshop on Cognitive Aspects of Computational Language Learning, pages 82–90,
Berlin, Germany, August 11, 2016. ©2016 Association for Computational Linguistics

performed other models of cross-situational word learning, including the model of Yu and Ballard (2007).

In a subsequent study which is the closest parallel to the problems dealt with in this paper, Frank et al. (2012) attempted to quantify the informativeness of eye gaze, hand positions and hand pointing (social cues), as well as referents of previous utterances (discourse continuity), using an ideal observer scenario. For each utterance, the toys present in the field of view of the child at the time of the utterance were coded. (To determine the timing, coders were listening to the audio.) The union of the sets of such objects associated with all the utterances of a video thus formed the set of possible referents. There were between 3 and 21 different objects per dyad, but the number of objects in the child's view (the ambiguity) for each utterance was on average between 1.18 and 2.93 per dyad. Then the object(s) in the context that were being looked at, held or pointed to by the parent (the social cues) were coded. In addition, the object(s) that were being looked at or held by the child (referred to as attentional cues) were coded. Finally, the parent's intended referent for each utterance — those that contained the name of an object or pronoun referring to it — were coded ("look at *the doggie*", "look at *his* eyes and ears").

The result, based on regarding each cue as a predictor for the object reference, was that pointing was a powerful predictor with a precision of 0.78. However, pointing was not frequently used; in other words, it had low recall in the sense that it was seldom used when an object was referred to (and instead other means were used). Eye gaze and hand position, on the other hand, had low prediction accuracies, with F-scores around 0.45. The result was that the social cues appeared to be noisy and that, generally speaking, no such cue on its own would allow an observer to resolve the referential ambiguities. Simulations with a supervised classifier indicated that the prediction accuracy could be somewhat improved by combining information from any two different cues, but that the third did not add anything.

As discussed by Frank et al. (2012), however, it is possible that some discriminatory power was lost because of the coarse temporal granularity of the model, where any temporal coordination below the utterance level was invisible. For example, if the parent was looking first at one object and later at another object during the same utterance, the coding did not capture the timing and ordering of these events. More generally, if there is a systematic timing relation between verbal and non-verbal cues that can support the learner's choice of referent, then we would want to distinguish it. A second limitation of the model was that all kinds of hand movements and gestures were coded as either of two discrete cues, namely, hand position and hand pointing.

This paper attempts to provide answers to two research questions arising out of this line of work: First, is it possible to obtain a more precise measure of the relative informativeness of the different social cues by adopting a more fine-grained model? Secondly, can we see any effects on informativeness in this model if we offset the timing of the non-verbal cues? In other words, is the timing actually used by the parents in some sense optimal with respect to the synchrony of verbal and non-verbal cues, or is the informativeness robust to (small) displacements of the cues forward or backward in time? To measure the information provided by social and attentional cues, we use a supervised classification method, and different assumptions about the length of short-term memory.

2 Data

This section describes our corpus and the annotation used to code the parents' and children's referential behaviour.

2.1 Corpus

Our primary data consist of audio and video recordings (using two cameras) from parent–child interaction in a recording studio at the Phonetics Laboratory at Stockholm University (Lacerda, 2009). The corpus consists of 18 parent–child dyads, totalling 7:29 hours, with three children each participating longitudinally in six dyads between the ages of seven and 33 months. The mean duration of a dyad is 24:58 minutes. The scenario was free play where the set of toys varied over time, but where two of them (the target objects) were present in all dyads.

2.2 Coding

All annotation of the corpus was made with the ELAN tool (Wittenburg et al., 2006) according to the guideline of Björkenstam and Wirén (2014), producing annotation cells on tiers time-aligned

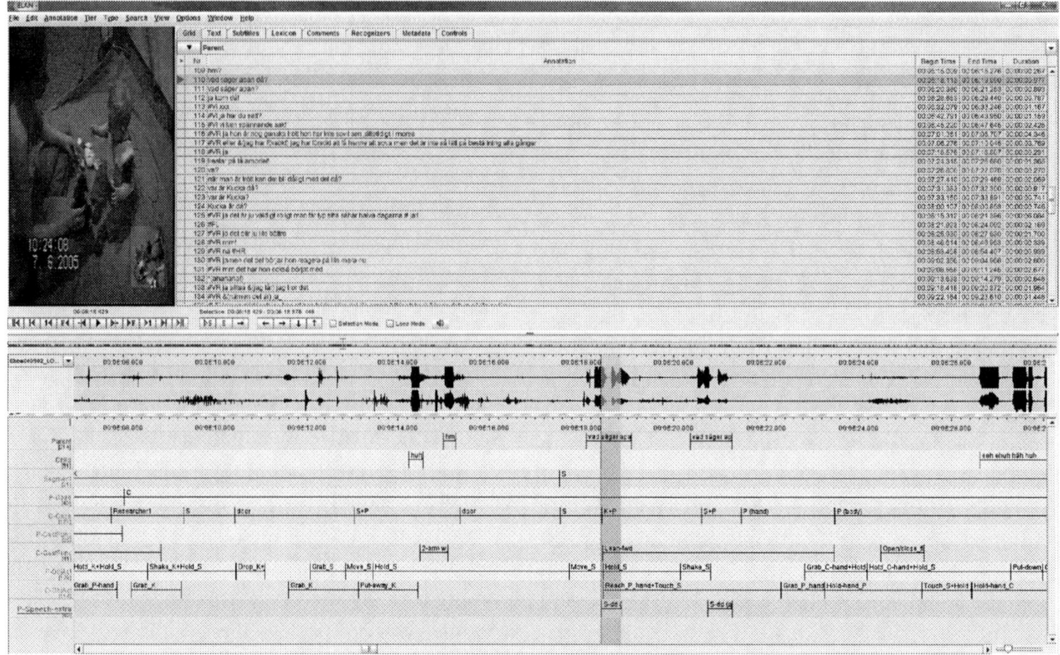

Figure 1: Screencap of ELAN annotation.

with the audio and video files (see Figure 1). The basic approach was to code each type of verbal and non-verbal referential event as well as the parent and child in separate tiers, thereby allowing for analysis separately and in different combinations.

First, for each dyad, the discourse segments in which a target object was in focus were coded by creating cells that spanned the corresponding timelines in a designated tier, annotated with the name of the focused object.[1] "Focus" here means that at least one of the participants' attention was directed to a target object,[2] and that, in the course of the segment, at least one verbal reference to the object was made by the parent. Such a segment was considered to end when the focus was shifted permanently to another (target or non-target) object.

These segments were then coded for verbal and non-verbal referential cues, involving speech, eye gaze, manual gesture, and manipulation of an object by (one or two) hands. The coding used cells spanning the timelines corresponding to the respective events in a separate tier for each type, and with separate tiers for the parent and child, thus re-

Table 2: Values of Cohen's Kappa (required overlap 0.6)

Annotation tier	Kappa
Parent's object manipulation	0.71
Child's object manipulation	0.75
Parent's eye gaze	0.60
Child's eye gaze	0.69

sulting in eight ELAN tiers overall. We took care in trying to recover information from each cue as objectively as possible. Accordingly, an important methodological consideration was that each tier was coded independently of the others in such a way that all the other tiers were hidden for the annotator.

The coding of speech involved all references to objects and persons present in the room by means of a name, definite description or pronoun. Each such reference was coded in an annotation cell spanning the timeline corresponding to the duration of the expression, with addition of its orthographic transcription and the speaker's intended referent. There were altogether 45 types of objects referred to verbally in the videos, but the distribution of these events was heavily skewed, mostly because of the prominent role of the two

---

[1] In some segments, both of the target objects were in focus and were then annotated with both names.

[2] Thus, there is not necessarily joint attention to the target object in the whole of such a segment.

Table 1: Number of occurrences of ten most frequent objects referred to verbally, ditto hand manipulations of objects, and ditto objects referred to non-verbally (using gaze or hand), all in decreasing order. P = parent, C = child, Siffu = target object 1, Kucka = target object 2.

Objects referred to verbally	Occur.	Hand manipulation	Occur.	Objects referred to non-verbally	Occur.
Siffu	377	hold	797	Siffu	1229
Kucka	275	reach	539	Kucka	1103
C	166	move	321	C	184
subS	29	show	262	bag-lid	173
subK	24	touch	217	bag	146
P	22	grab	165	P	66
dress-white	14	pick-up	143	dress-white	61
bib	11	explore	120	bottle	55
car	11	enact	114	dress-pink	42
wire	8	shake	95	brush	36

target objects. The most frequently referred objects are shown in the two leftmost columns of Table 1. As seen in the table, only three objects were referred to more than 30 times: target object 1 (called Siffu), target object 2 (Kucka) and child.

As for non-verbal references, the coding of gaze similarly consisted of a cell spanning the timeline of the act, with a specification of the object looked at. If two objects were joined together in the field of view of an agent, the object looked at was coded as the larger of them. For example, if the parent was looking at the child holding a car, we would code this as the child being the subject of the gaze.

In the coding of manual object manipulation, we wanted to capture the large variation in how the parent and child were handling the objects. We thus distinguished 79 types of object manipulation acts, which again turned out to occur in a skewed distribution as shown in the two middle columns in Table 1. Altogether, there were 85 different objects referred to non-verbally (using gaze or hand), of which the most frequent ones are shown in the two rightmost columns in Table 1. Manual gesture occurred very infrequently (and only for the purpose of deictic pointing), and was not used in the subsequent analysis.

The use of timelines in ELAN allows for a high temporal resolution, permitting us to track the information from the cues very precisely. The high resolution also brings technical challenges, however; while Frank et al. (2012) could assume a discrete-time setting and simply use a model pre-

Table 3: Tuples extracted from coding of gaze. P = parent, C = child, Siffu = target object 1, Kucka = target object 2

Element	Values
Predicate	gaze
Agent	P, C
Patient	Siffu, Kucka, C, bag-lid, bag, P, ...

dicting referents from all the events observed during an entire utterance, we need a continuous-time model to fully exploit the information from our coding.

The reliability of the coding scheme was evaluated by comparing the output by two annotators on two representative dyads, using the built-in ELAN function for calculating Cohen's Kappa (see Table 2). Reliability was high for children's eye gaze as well as object manipulation by parent and child (around 0.7), but slightly lower for parent eye gaze (0.6).

3 Method

While the child has access to a vast amount of information from different senses (including touch, taste, smell, etc.), as well as memories from before the recording session, the goal of our simulated learner is to predict which object is being referred to given nothing but the information from the different cues. We assume, however, that our learner knows how to segment continuous speech

Table 4: Tuples extracted from coding of hand manipulation of object. P = parent, C = child, `Siffu` = target object 1, `Kucka` = target object 2

Element	Values
Predicate	`hold, reach, move, show,` ...
Agent	`P, C`
Patient	`Siffu, Kucka, C, bag-lid,` `bag, P,` ...

into utterances and words, that it can perceive and represent objects in the physical context, and that it is sensitive to the interlocutor's gaze. We furthermore assume that the learner simulates the *beginnings* of lexical acquisition in the sense that the only information provided by the speech is *that* some object in the context is being referred to verbally, but nothing related to the meaning of the words.

To provide a measure of the information inherent in the cues, we use a supervised classification method. Following Frank et al. (2012), we thus use classification accuracy as a proxy for the variable we are really interested in, namely, the informativeness of different cues. Highly informative cues provide relatively unambiguous information about the referent, and a reasonable classifier should then be able to identify the referent with a high level of accuracy.

It would also be possible to use the perplexity or, equivalently, likelihood of the test data in order to compare different models. This would capture the (un)certainty of each model, rather than just its ability to predict the correct referent. While intuitively appealing, this would increase the influence of uninteresting model parameters (such as regularization strength) on the result, so for this reason we stick to the more easily interpretable measure of plain classification accuracy.

As features for the classifier, we extracted information from the coding which we represent as tuples. Thus, for gaze, we extract triples consisting of ⟨`gaze`, *agent*, *patient*⟩, as shown in Table 3. For object manipulation we extracted triples in the format ⟨*predicate*, *agent*, *patient*⟩, for example, ⟨`pick-up, C, car`⟩. As mentioned in Section 2.2, there were 79 different values for *predicate* and 85 different values for *patient*; the most frequent ones of these are shown in Table 4.[3] We

also keep track of the timing information for each mention and each gaze- or hand-related cue.

The particular task that our model solves is a multinomial classification between the possible referents at time t, which we choose to coincide with the start of a mention by the parent. For this, we use a multinomial logistic regression (Maximum Entropy) model with predictors that depend on the type of event as well as the time passed since the event finished.

Each combination of values in a tuple that encodes a non-verbal event, such as ⟨`gaze, P, car`⟩ or ⟨`pick-up, C, car`⟩, corresponds to a feature in the model. To compute the value of this feature at time t, we use an exponential decay function to simulate short-term memory. The memory equation has the form $f(t) = e^{-kt}$, where k is a constant that determines the length (half-life) of the memory, and t is defined by

$$t = t_{mention}^{start} - t_{event}^{end}$$

where $t_{mention}^{start}$ is the time at which the mention starts and t_{event}^{end} is the time at which the non-verbal event ends, or $t = 0$ in case these two overlap. Ongoing non-verbal events are defined to have a value of 1, but as soon as the non-verbal event ends, the decay begins. In case the non-verbal event and mention overlap, the event will have a value of 1, according to the memory equation. Future events (that is, events that have not yet occurred) are defined to have a value of 0.[4]

As mentioned in Section 2.2, the distributions of predicates and objects ware skewed. To avoid having a lot of unusual features in the model, we therefore used one threshold for inclusion of verbal mentions, which we set to 100, and one threshold for the use by the classifier of unique triples representing object manipulations, which we set to 10. The rationale for the lower threshold is that the classifier is robust to some noise, but only if there is a sufficient number of instances for the predicting variable (verbal mentions), hence the higher threshold in that case. Consequently, only the three most frequently mentioned objects were used in the classification.

---

[3] Sometimes one predicate was associated with several patients, for example, ⟨`gaze, C,` ⟨`car, Siffu`⟩⟩. In this case, two features were generated with the same timestamps: ⟨`gaze, C, car`⟩ and ⟨`gaze, C, Siffu`⟩.

[4] If we would like to put more emphasis on changes of state, it is possible to include decay during an event as well to down-weigh the information from this event once the novelty wears off.

Table 5: Results of experiment 1. Accuracy (in percent) of model prediction given type of cue. Columns show from which agents information is incorporated into the model (P = parent, C = child, P + C = both). The upper half shows results from our model as described, the lower half uses the same data but only utterance-level binary features, thus emulating the model of Frank et al. (2012).

Type of cue used	P	C	P + C
Fine-grained temporal information			
Hand	72.9	71.8	82.5
Gaze	75.8	80.8	84.2
Hand + gaze	81.7	83.6	88.7
Utterance-level temporal information			
Hand	61.5	64.1	66.6
Gaze	61.4	59.8	62.3
Hand + gaze	64.4	65.0	69.5

We train and evaluate the model using a leave-one-out strategy on the recording session level, so that we fit as many models as there are recording sessions (18). Each model is fitted using data from all but one session, then used to predict the referents of the remaining session. This method allows us to use as much as possible of the available data, while at the same time avoiding session-specific context to influence the model.

4 Experiments

This section describes how we used our model in three experiments to try to measure the informativeness and timing of non-verbal cues.

Experiment 1: Informativeness of non-verbal cues

First, we were interested in obtaining measures of the informativeness of the non-verbal cues from both the parent and child as seen from a third-person observer (in effect, looking at their joint interaction), as well as from the agents as seen separately. To this end, we trained classifiers on cues including gaze and hand manipulation for the input from each agent as well as from both of them. For this experiment, we used the two target objects as referents. We did not include the child, because the objective here was to use external information sources as seen from the parent and child, and we did not include any other objects for lack of data. The half-life of the short-term memory

Table 6: Results of experiment 2. Accuracy (in percent) of model prediction per referent.

	Precision	Recall	F-score
C	31.0	13.3	18.6
Kucka	69.0	74.5	71.7
Siffu	73.6	87.8	80.0

decay used here was 3 seconds. The baseline is given by the most frequently referred one, target object 1 (Siffu), which was used in 58% of the cases. An uninformed model could thus achieve an accuracy of 58% by always predicting Siffu.

Table 5 shows the accuracy of the model's predictions given different cue combinations and information sources (agents). Overall, the differences in predictive accuracy between the various cue combinations are fairly small, but we can note some things. First, gaze turns out to be more informative than hand manipulation of objects. Secondly, a comparison of the P and C columns shows that roughly the same amount of information is provided by both agents, indicating a high degree of convergence in their interaction.

For comparison, we also include at the end of table 5 the corresponding accuracies obtained using the paradigm of Frank et al. (2012), that is, discarding our fine-grained temporal information and using only utterance-level binary features. The result is a sharp decline in prediction accuracy. It is noteworthy that gaze comes out as less informative than hand manipulation under these circumstances, which is consistent with the results reported by Frank et al. The relative importance of cues thus seems to depend strongly on the resolution of the temporal information available to the model.

Finally, we can see that the prediction accuracy is higher when the information sources are combined, as we would expect. The P + C column shows that the prediction accuracy of a third person view classifier (trained on both parent and child input) is consistently higher than the accuracy of the classifiers trained on input from P and C, respectively.

Experiment 2: Informativeness of non-verbal cues to known referents

In the second experiment, we were interested in determining if there were differences in informativess of non-verbal cues that depended on the object referred to. This question may bear upon problems related to givenness and accessibility in the domain. In each dyad, the child is a second-person referent, and the target objects are third-person referents. For example, according to Ariel (1999), second-person referents are consistently highly accessible, whereas third-person referents are highly accessible only when they constitute the discourse topic. Our model thus permits us to investigate whether there are differences in the informativity of non-verbal cues with respect to second- and third-person referents. Since the number of references to the child was exceeded only by the target objects, we therefore included this as a third object.

For this experiment, we thus trained classifiers on cues including gaze and hand manipulation for the input from both agents combined. Table 6 shows that predicting the child is much more difficult than the external (target) objects. Using gaze and action information from both participants, we achieve F-scores of 71.6% and 80.0% for the two toys, but only 18.6% for the child.

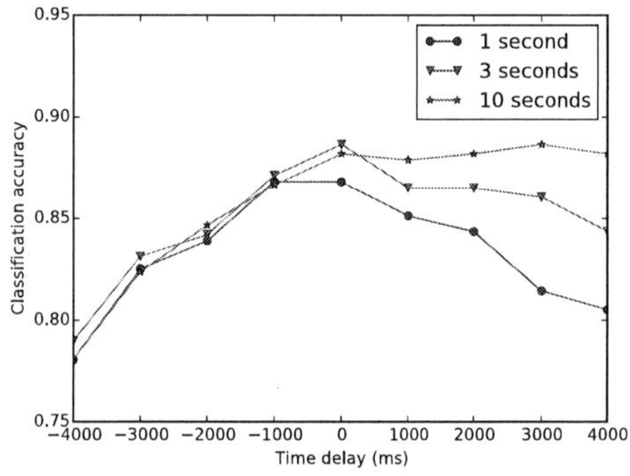

Figure 2: Results of experiment 3. Classification accuracy (y-axis) as a function of verbal mention, offset whole seconds from actual word occurrence in parent speech up/down to ± 4 seconds (x-axis), given a short-term memory of 1, 3, and 10 seconds, respectively. Time = 0 coincides with the start of the mentions by the parent.

Experiment 3: Timing of non-verbal cues

Our final experiment concerned the timing of non-verbal cues. Previous research has highlighted the time-synchronicity of non-verbal cues with verbal utterances (Matatyaho and Gogate, 2008; Lacerda, 2009). Furthermore, there has been work in the HSP paradigm on determining the effects to referential transparency by displacing these cues (Trueswell et al., 2016). Using our fine-grained representation of time, we wanted to investigate the effects in our model to see if would arrive at similar effects as Trueswell et al.

Our hypothesis was that non-verbal cues are synchronised with speech, and that displacing the verbal mention from its actual temporal position in the input would lead to a drop in classifier performance. We tested this by training a classifier on input where the timing of the predictions relative to the onset of speech had been moved by whole seconds up/down to ± 4 seconds. This is comparable to displacing the speech relative to the non-verbal event with the same amount of time. We also explored how short-term memory decay influenced classification accuracy by comparing three classifiers with a memory half-life of 1, 3 and 10 seconds, respectively.

The effects of the timing displacement on accuracy appear in Figure 2. The 0 second verbal mention offset is the baseline, with an accuracy of about 86% for the 1 second memory model, and around 88% for the 3 and 10 second memory models. Accuracy dropped when verbal mention offset was displaced. Moving the verbal mention offset ahead in time by as little as two seconds resulted in accuracy scores of 82% for the 1 second model, and 84% for the 3 and 10 second memory models. Delaying the verbal mention by 2 seconds had a less detrimental effect, in particular for the 10 second model.

5 Discussion

The goal of this study was to develop a model for fine-grained measuring of the informativeness and effects of displaced timing of non-verbal cues in parent–child interaction. To this end, we used a corpus of videos of child-directed interaction in a free-play setting involving several objects, but where most of the interaction was centred on two target objects. We coded the segments of the interaction that were focused on these objects with verbal and non-verbal references, using speech, gaze and hand manipulation of objects for this study. To obtain a measure of the informativeness of different cues, we used classification accuracy of the different referents.

The main difference with respect to the model of Frank et al. (2012) concerns the representation of time. Frank et al. use a discrete-time setting in which a referent is predicted from all the events observed during an entire utterance. In contrast, our model uses a continuous-time representation working off the coding along ELAN timelines. A further difference is that our model includes a simulation of short-term memory decay, where the value of a feature is 1 if it occurs at the time of the mention (the noun phrase), and then decreases exponentially.

Another kind of difference concerns the way in which we represent non-verbal cues. Frank et al. also investigated cues associated with speech, gaze and hand, but for the latter they only used binary features consisting of one discrete cue for hand position and hand pointing, respectively. Our coding is more feature-rich, distinguishing 79 types of hand manipulation.

On the other hand, Frank et al. have a broader perspective in the sense that they also model discourse continuity; in other words, the fact that in the absence of contradicting information, it is most likely that what is being talked about now is the same thing as what was talked about a moment ago. We also do not take prosody into account, as is done by Yu and Ballard (2007).

Our first experiment concerned the relative informativeness of non-verbal cues for word-referent mapping. We found that gaze is the most informative cue, which is inconsistent with the study of Frank et al. In particular, child gaze was highly informative. We interpret this as evidence of the parent's ability to recognise the focus of the child's attention, and to create and maintain joint attention. Additional support for our hypothesis is given by the fact that non-verbal cues, and gaze in particular, became much less informative when we emulated Frank et al.'s experimental setup by discarding temporal information for our classifier.

The third person view classifier, trained on both parent and child input, achieved the highest accuracy. Although we do not have any direct coding of joint attention, it seems that to some degree the third person view classifier captured instances of joint attention through the coding of gaze and object manipulation.

In our second experiment, we compared the informativeness of non-verbal cues to mentions of a second person referent (the child) with mentions of third person referents (the target objects). We found that this task is more complex than classification of mentions of third person referents. These results raise the question whether non-verbal cues are used less when the speaker assumes that the referent of a word is known to the listener. In this case, the parent knows that the child already knows his/her name, and thus references to the child may be used mainly as means of getting the attention of the child.

In our third experiment, we tested the hypothesis that non-verbal cues are synchronous with speech by displacing the verbal mention from its temporal position in the input. We expected a drop in classifier performance, and found that especially negative offsets resulted in lower accuracy. We found an assymmetry in the effect of timing that is similar to experimental results on timing by Trueswell et al. (2016, p. 128), who note that "the greatest changes in cues to referential intent occur just before, rather than after, word onset [. . .]; moving the beep [that is, word onset] early effectively causes these events to happen too late to be perceived as causally related to the linguistic event".

6 Conclusions

Our findings show that gaze is the single most important non-verbal cue for predicting external object referents, thereby contradicting the study of Frank et al. (2012). We attribute the difference to our addition of fine-grained temporal information, as we can compare our results to those of Frank et al. by simulating their time resolution. Another result is that that non-verbal cues seem much more informative for predicting third-person than second-person references. Finally, we have demonstrated the importance of synchrony by showing that displacing the verbal mention in time degrades prediction accuracy, particularly when the offset is negative. This is consistent with the findings of Trueswell et al. (2016, Figure 2, and compare our Figure 2) who instead of a statistical classifier working off the annotation used human observers of the video.

Acknowledgements

This research is part of the project "Modelling the emergence of linguistic structures in early childhood", funded by the Swedish Research Council as 2011-675-86010-31. We would like to thank (in chronological order) Anna Ericsson, Joel Petersson Ivre, Johan Sjons, Lisa Tengstrand, and Annika Schwittek for annotation work, and the three anonymous reviewers for valuable comments.

References

Mira Ariel. 1999. The development of person agreement markers: From pronouns to higher accessibility markers. In M. Barlow and S. Kemmer, editors, *Usage-based Models of Language*, pages 197–260. Stanford, California: CSLI Publications.

K.N. Björkenstam and M. Wirén. 2014. Multimodal annotation of synchrony in longitudinal parent–child interaction. In J. Edlund, D. Heylen, and P. Paggio, editors, *MMC 2014 Multimodal Corpora: Combining applied and basic research targets: Workshop at The 9th edition of the Language Resources and Evaluation Conference*. ELRA.

M.C. Frank, N.D. Goodman, and J.B. Tenenbaum. 2009. Using speakers' referential intentions to model early cross-situational word learning. *Psychological Science*, 20(5):578–585.

M.C. Frank, J.B. Tenenbaum, and A. Fernald. 2012. Social and discourse contributions to the determination of reference in cross-situational learning. *Language Learning and Development*, pages 1–24.

Wilson S. Geisler. 2011. Contributions of ideal observer theory to vision research. *Vision Research*, 51(7):771–781. Vision Research 50th Anniversary Issue: Part 1.

J. Gillette, H. Gleitman, L. Gleitman, and A. Lederer. 1999. Human simulations of vocabulary learning. *Cognition*, 73:135—176.

L.J. Gogate, L.H. Bolzani, and E.A. Betancourt. 2006. Attention to maternal multimodal naming by 6- to 8-month-old infants and learning of word-object relations. *Infancy*, 9:259–288.

Francisco Lacerda. 2009. On the emergence of early linguistic functions: A biologic and interactional perspective. In *Brain Talk: Discourse with and in the brain*, number 1 in Birgit Rausing Language Program Conference in Linguistics, pages 207–230. Media-Tryck.

D.J. Matatyaho and L.J. Gogate. 2008. Type of maternal object motion during synchronous naming predicts preverbal infants' learning of word-object relations. *Infancy*, 13:172–184.

T.N. Medina, J. Snedeker, J.C. Trueswell, and L. Gleitman. 2011. How words can and cannot be learned by observation. *PNAS*, 108(22):9014–9019.

T.B. Piccin and S.R. Waxman. 2007. Why nouns trump verbs in word learning: New evidence from children and adults in the human simulation paradigm. *Language Learning and Development*, 3(4):295–323.

M. Tomasello. 2000. The social-pragmatic theory of word learning. *Pragmatics*, 10(4):401–413.

J.C. Trueswell, Y. Lin, B. Armstrong III, E.A. Cartmill, S. Goldin-Meadow, and L.R. Gleitman. 2016. Perceiving referential intent: Dynamics of reference in natural parent-child interactions. *Cognition*, 148:117–135.

P. Wittenburg, H. Brugman, A. Russel, A. Klassmann, and H. Sloetjes. 2006. ELAN: A Professional Framework for Multimodality Research. In *Proceedings of LREC 2006, Fifth International Conference on Language Resources and Evaluation*. ELRA.

C. Yu and D.H. Ballard. 2007. A unified model of early world learning: Integrating statistical and social cues. *Neurocomputing*, 70:2149–2165.

Author Index